I0329807

C-4784 CAREER EXAMINATION SERIES

This is your PASSBOOK for...

Office Assistant III (Calculations)

Test Preparation Study Guide
Questions & Answers

NLC®

NATIONAL LEARNING CORPORATION®

COPYRIGHT NOTICE

National Learning Corporation

212 Michael Drive, Syosset, NY 11791
(516) 921-8888 • www.passbooks.com
E-mail: info@passbooks.com

PASSBOOK® SERIES

THE *PASSBOOK® SERIES* has been created to prepare applicants and candidates for the ultimate academic battlefield – the examination room.

At some time in our lives, each and every one of us may be required to take an examination – for validation, matriculation, admission, qualification, registration, certification, or licensure.

Based on the assumption that every applicant or candidate has met the basic formal educational standards, has taken the required number of courses, and read the necessary texts, the *PASSBOOK® SERIES* furnishes the one special preparation which may assure passing with confidence, instead of failing with insecurity. Examination questions – together with answers – are furnished as the basic vehicle for study so that the mysteries of the examination and its compounding difficulties may be eliminated or diminished by a sure method.

This book is meant to help you pass your examination provided that you qualify and are serious in your objective.

The entire field is reviewed through the huge store of content information which is succinctly presented through a provocative and challenging approach – the question-and-answer method.

A climate of success is established by furnishing the correct answers at the end of each test.

You soon learn to recognize types of questions, forms of questions, and patterns of questioning. You may even begin to anticipate expected outcomes.

You perceive that many questions are repeated or adapted so that you can gain acute insights, which may enable you to score many sure points.

You learn how to confront new questions, or types of questions, and to attack them confidently and work out the correct answers.

You note objectives and emphases, and recognize pitfalls and dangers, so that you may make positive educational adjustments.

Moreover, you are kept fully informed in relation to new concepts, methods, practices, and directions in the field.

You discover that you are actually taking the examination all the time: you are preparing for the examination by "taking" an examination, not by reading extraneous and/or supererogatory textbooks.

In short, this PASSBOOK®, used directedly, should be an important factor in helping you to pass your test.

OFFICE ASSISTANT III (CALCULATIONS)

DUTIES:

As an **Office Assistant III (Calculations)**, you would spend most of your time supervising mathematical operations, and/or clerical activities related to mathematical operations. These activities may include creating spreadsheets, using calculators, and retrieving information from various computer databases, including the Statewide Financial System and/or Microsoft Access or similar computer database software package. The duties may incorporate, but are not limited to, financial (including record-keeping, bookkeeping, and reconciliation activities), purchasing, or statistical functions. Positions at this level act as the head of a clerical operation, typically functioning as second-level supervisor.

SUBJECT OF EXAMINATION:

The written test is designed to test for knowledge, skills, and/or abilities in such areas as:

1. **Office management** - These questions test for knowledge of the principles and practices of planning, organizing, and controlling the activities of an office and directing those performing office activities so as to achieve predetermined objectives such as accomplishing office work within reasonable limits of time, effort, and cost expenditure. Typical activities may include but will not be restricted to: simplifying and improving procedures, increasing office efficiency, improving the office work environment, and controlling office supplies.
2. **Supervision** - These questions test for knowledge of the principles and practices employed in planning, organizing, and controlling the activities of a work unit toward predetermined objectives. The concepts covered, usually in a situational question format, include such topics as assigning and reviewing work; evaluating performance; maintaining work standards; motivating and developing subordinates; implementing procedural change; increasing efficiency; and dealing with problems of absenteeism, morale, and discipline.
3. **Understanding and interpreting written material** - These questions test for the ability to understand and interpret written material. You will be presented with brief reading passages and will be asked questions about the passages. You should base your answers to the questions only on what is presented in the passages and not on what you may happen to know about the topic.
4. **Understanding and interpreting tabular material** - These questions test your ability to understand, analyze, and use the internal logic of data presented in tabular form. You may be asked to perform tasks such as completing tables, drawing conclusions from them, analyzing data trends or interrelationships, and revising or combining data sets. The concepts of rate, ratio, and proportion are tested. Mathematical operations are simple, and computational speed is not a major factor in the test.

OFFICE ASSISTANT (IMPLICATIONS)

HOW TO TAKE A TEST

I. YOU MUST PASS AN EXAMINATION

A. WHAT EVERY CANDIDATE SHOULD KNOW

Examination applicants often ask us for help in preparing for the written test. What can I study in advance? What kinds of questions will be asked? How will the test be given? How will the papers be graded?

As an applicant for a civil service examination, you may be wondering about some of these things. Our purpose here is to suggest effective methods of advance study and to describe civil service examinations.

Your chances for success on this examination can be increased if you know how to prepare. Those "pre-examination jitters" can be reduced if you know what to expect. You can even experience an adventure in good citizenship if you know why civil service exams are given.

B. WHY ARE CIVIL SERVICE EXAMINATIONS GIVEN?

Civil service examinations are important to you in two ways. As a citizen, you want public jobs filled by employees who know how to do their work. As a job seeker, you want a fair chance to compete for that job on an equal footing with other candidates. The best-known means of accomplishing this two-fold goal is the competitive examination.

Exams are widely publicized throughout the nation. They may be administered for jobs in federal, state, city, municipal, town or village governments or agencies.

Any citizen may apply, with some limitations, such as the age or residence of applicants. Your experience and education may be reviewed to see whether you meet the requirements for the particular examination. When these requirements exist, they are reasonable and applied consistently to all applicants. Thus, a competitive examination may cause you some uneasiness now, but it is your privilege and safeguard.

C. HOW ARE CIVIL SERVICE EXAMS DEVELOPED?

Examinations are carefully written by trained technicians who are specialists in the field known as "psychological measurement," in consultation with recognized authorities in the field of work that the test will cover. These experts recommend the subject matter areas or skills to be tested; only those knowledges or skills important to your success on the job are included. The most reliable books and source materials available are used as references. Together, the experts and technicians judge the difficulty level of the questions.

Test technicians know how to phrase questions so that the problem is clearly stated. Their ethics do not permit "trick" or "catch" questions. Questions may have been tried out on sample groups, or subjected to statistical analysis, to determine their usefulness.

Written tests are often used in combination with performance tests, ratings of training and experience, and oral interviews. All of these measures combine to form the best-known means of finding the right person for the right job.

II. HOW TO PASS THE WRITTEN TEST

A. NATURE OF THE EXAMINATION

To prepare intelligently for civil service examinations, you should know how they differ from school examinations you have taken. In school you were assigned certain definite pages to read or subjects to cover. The examination questions were quite detailed and usually emphasized memory. Civil service exams, on the other hand, try to discover your present ability to perform the duties of a position, plus your potentiality to learn these duties. In other words, a civil service exam attempts to predict how successful you will be. Questions cover such a broad area that they cannot be as minute and detailed as school exam questions.

In the public service similar kinds of work, or positions, are grouped together in one "class." This process is known as *position-classification.* All the positions in a class are paid according to the salary range for that class. One class title covers all of these positions, and they are all tested by the same examination.

B. FOUR BASIC STEPS

1) Study the announcement

How, then, can you know what subjects to study? Our best answer is: "Learn as much as possible about the class of positions for which you've applied." The exam will test the knowledge, skills and abilities needed to do the work.

Your most valuable source of information about the position you want is the official exam announcement. This announcement lists the training and experience qualifications. Check these standards and apply only if you come reasonably close to meeting them.

The brief description of the position in the examination announcement offers some clues to the subjects which will be tested. Think about the job itself. Review the duties in your mind. Can you perform them, or are there some in which you are rusty? Fill in the blank spots in your preparation.

Many jurisdictions preview the written test in the exam announcement by including a section called "Knowledge and Abilities Required," "Scope of the Examination," or some similar heading. Here you will find out specifically what fields will be tested.

2) Review your own background

Once you learn in general what the position is all about, and what you need to know to do the work, ask yourself which subjects you already know fairly well and which need improvement. You may wonder whether to concentrate on improving your strong areas or on building some background in your fields of weakness. When the announcement has specified "some knowledge" or "considerable knowledge," or has used adjectives like "beginning principles of..." or "advanced ... methods," you can get a clue as to the number and difficulty of questions to be asked in any given field. More questions, and hence broader coverage, would be included for those subjects which are more important in the work. Now weigh your strengths and weaknesses against the job requirements and prepare accordingly.

3) Determine the level of the position

Another way to tell how intensively you should prepare is to understand the level of the job for which you are applying. Is it the entering level? In other words, is this the position in which beginners in a field of work are hired? Or is it an intermediate or advanced level? Sometimes this is indicated by such words as "Junior" or "Senior" in the class title. Other jurisdictions use Roman numerals to designate the level – Clerk I, Clerk II, for example. The word "Supervisor" sometimes appears in the title. If the level is not indicated by the title, check the description of duties. Will you be working under very close supervision, or will you have responsibility for independent decisions in this work?

4) Choose appropriate study materials

Now that you know the subjects to be examined and the relative amount of each subject to be covered, you can choose suitable study materials. For beginning level jobs, or even advanced ones, if you have a pronounced weakness in some aspect of your training, read a modern, standard textbook in that field. Be sure it is up to date and has general coverage. Such books are normally available at your library, and the librarian will be glad to help you locate one. For entry-level positions, questions of appropriate difficulty are chosen – neither highly advanced questions, nor those too simple. Such questions require careful thought but not advanced training.

If the position for which you are applying is technical or advanced, you will read more advanced, specialized material. If you are already familiar with the basic principles of your field, elementary textbooks would waste your time. Concentrate on advanced textbooks and technical periodicals. Think through the concepts and review difficult problems in your field.

These are all general sources. You can get more ideas on your own initiative, following these leads. For example, training manuals and publications of the government agency which employs workers in your field can be useful, particularly for technical and professional positions. A letter or visit to the government department involved may result in more specific study suggestions, and certainly will provide you with a more definite idea of the exact nature of the position you are seeking.

III. KINDS OF TESTS

Tests are used for purposes other than measuring knowledge and ability to perform specified duties. For some positions, it is equally important to test ability to make adjustments to new situations or to profit from training. In others, basic mental abilities not dependent on information are essential. Questions which test these things may not appear as pertinent to the duties of the position as those which test for knowledge and information. Yet they are often highly important parts of a fair examination. For very general questions, it is almost impossible to help you direct your study efforts. What we can do is to point out some of the more common of these general abilities needed in public service positions and describe some typical questions.

1) General information

Broad, general information has been found useful for predicting job success in some kinds of work. This is tested in a variety of ways, from vocabulary lists to questions about current events. Basic background in some field of work, such as sociology or economics, may be sampled in a group of questions. Often these are principles which have become familiar to most persons through exposure rather than through formal training. It is difficult to advise you how to study for these questions; being alert to the world around you is our best suggestion.

2) Verbal ability

An example of an ability needed in many positions is verbal or language ability. Verbal ability is, in brief, the ability to use and understand words. Vocabulary and grammar tests are typical measures of this ability. Reading comprehension or paragraph interpretation questions are common in many kinds of civil service tests. You are given a paragraph of written material and asked to find its central meaning.

3) Numerical ability

Number skills can be tested by the familiar arithmetic problem, by checking paired lists of numbers to see which are alike and which are different, or by interpreting charts and graphs. In the latter test, a graph may be printed in the test booklet which you are asked to use as the basis for answering questions.

4) Observation

A popular test for law-enforcement positions is the observation test. A picture is shown to you for several minutes, then taken away. Questions about the picture test your ability to observe both details and larger elements.

5) Following directions

In many positions in the public service, the employee must be able to carry out written instructions dependably and accurately. You may be given a chart with several columns, each column listing a variety of information. The questions require you to carry out directions involving the information given in the chart.

6) Skills and aptitudes

Performance tests effectively measure some manual skills and aptitudes. When the skill is one in which you are trained, such as typing or shorthand, you can practice. These tests are often very much like those given in business school or high school courses. For many of the other skills and aptitudes, however, no short-time preparation can be made. Skills and abilities natural to you or that you have developed throughout your lifetime are being tested.

Many of the general questions just described provide all the data needed to answer the questions and ask you to use your reasoning ability to find the answers. Your best preparation for these tests, as well as for tests of facts and ideas, is to be at your physical and mental best. You, no doubt, have your own methods of getting into an exam-taking mood and keeping "in shape." The next section lists some ideas on this subject.

IV. KINDS OF QUESTIONS

Only rarely is the "essay" question, which you answer in narrative form, used in civil service tests. Civil service tests are usually of the short-answer type. Full instructions for answering these questions will be given to you at the examination. But in case this is your first experience with short-answer questions and separate answer sheets, here is what you need to know:

1) Multiple-choice Questions

Most popular of the short-answer questions is the "multiple choice" or "best answer" question. It can be used, for example, to test for factual knowledge, ability to solve problems or judgment in meeting situations found at work.

A multiple-choice question is normally one of three types—

- It can begin with an incomplete statement followed by several possible endings. You are to find the one ending which *best* completes the statement, although some of the others may not be entirely wrong.
- It can also be a complete statement in the form of a question which is answered by choosing one of the statements listed.

- It can be in the form of a problem – again you select the best answer.

Here is an example of a multiple-choice question with a discussion which should give you some clues as to the method for choosing the right answer:

When an employee has a complaint about his assignment, the action which will *best* help him overcome his difficulty is to

A. discuss his difficulty with his coworkers
B. take the problem to the head of the organization
C. take the problem to the person who gave him the assignment
D. say nothing to anyone about his complaint

In answering this question, you should study each of the choices to find which is best. Consider choice "A" – Certainly an employee may discuss his complaint with fellow employees, but no change or improvement can result, and the complaint remains unresolved. Choice "B" is a poor choice since the head of the organization probably does not know what assignment you have been given, and taking your problem to him is known as "going over the head" of the supervisor. The supervisor, or person who made the assignment, is the person who can clarify it or correct any injustice. Choice "C" is, therefore, correct. To say nothing, as in choice "D," is unwise. Supervisors have and interest in knowing the problems employees are facing, and the employee is seeking a solution to his problem.

2) True/False Questions

The "true/false" or "right/wrong" form of question is sometimes used. Here a complete statement is given. Your job is to decide whether the statement is right or wrong.

SAMPLE: A roaming cell-phone call to a nearby city costs less than a non-roaming call to a distant city.

This statement is wrong, or false, since roaming calls are more expensive.

This is not a complete list of all possible question forms, although most of the others are variations of these common types. You will always get complete directions for answering questions. Be sure you understand *how* to mark your answers – ask questions until you do.

V. RECORDING YOUR ANSWERS

Computer terminals are used more and more today for many different kinds of exams.

For an examination with very few applicants, you may be told to record your answers in the test booklet itself. Separate answer sheets are much more common. If this separate answer sheet is to be scored by machine – and this is often the case – it is highly important that you mark your answers correctly in order to get credit.

An electronic scoring machine is often used in civil service offices because of the speed with which papers can be scored. Machine-scored answer sheets must be marked with a pencil, which will be given to you. This pencil has a high graphite content which responds to the electronic scoring machine. As a matter of fact, stray dots may register as answers, so do not let your pencil rest on the answer sheet while you are pondering the correct answer. Also, if your pencil lead breaks or is otherwise defective, ask for another.

Since the answer sheet will be dropped in a slot in the scoring machine, be careful not to bend the corners or get the paper crumpled.

The answer sheet normally has five vertical columns of numbers, with 30 numbers to a column. These numbers correspond to the question numbers in your test booklet. After each number, going across the page are four or five pairs of dotted lines. These short dotted lines have small letters or numbers above them. The first two pairs may also have a "T" or "F" above the letters. This indicates that the first two pairs only are to be used if the questions are of the true-false type. If the questions are multiple choice, disregard the "T" and "F" and pay attention only to the small letters or numbers.

Answer your questions in the manner of the sample that follows:

32. The largest city in the United States is
    - A. Washington, D.C.
    - B. New York City
    - C. Chicago
    - D. Detroit
    - E. San Francisco

1) Choose the answer you think is best. (New York City is the largest, so "B" is correct.)
2) Find the row of dotted lines numbered the same as the question you are answering. (Find row number 32)
3) Find the pair of dotted lines corresponding to the answer. (Find the pair of lines under the mark "B.")
4) Make a solid black mark between the dotted lines.

VI. BEFORE THE TEST

Common sense will help you find procedures to follow to get ready for an examination. Too many of us, however, overlook these sensible measures. Indeed, nervousness and fatigue have been found to be the most serious reasons why applicants fail to do their best on civil service tests. Here is a list of reminders:

- Begin your preparation early – Don't wait until the last minute to go scurrying around for books and materials or to find out what the position is all about.
- Prepare continuously – An hour a night for a week is better than an all-night cram session. This has been definitely established. What is more, a night a week for a month will return better dividends than crowding your study into a shorter period of time.
- Locate the place of the exam – You have been sent a notice telling you when and where to report for the examination. If the location is in a different town or otherwise unfamiliar to you, it would be well to inquire the best route and learn something about the building.
- Relax the night before the test – Allow your mind to rest. Do not study at all that night. Plan some mild recreation or diversion; then go to bed early and get a good night's sleep.
- Get up early enough to make a leisurely trip to the place for the test – This way unforeseen events, traffic snarls, unfamiliar buildings, etc. will not upset you.
- Dress comfortably – A written test is not a fashion show. You will be known by number and not by name, so wear something comfortable.

- Leave excess paraphernalia at home – Shopping bags and odd bundles will get in your way. You need bring only the items mentioned in the official notice you received; usually everything you need is provided. Do not bring reference books to the exam. They will only confuse those last minutes and be taken away from you when in the test room.
- Arrive somewhat ahead of time – If because of transportation schedules you must get there very early, bring a newspaper or magazine to take your mind off yourself while waiting.
- Locate the examination room – When you have found the proper room, you will be directed to the seat or part of the room where you will sit. Sometimes you are given a sheet of instructions to read while you are waiting. Do not fill out any forms until you are told to do so; just read them and be prepared.
- Relax and prepare to listen to the instructions
- If you have any physical problem that may keep you from doing your best, be sure to tell the test administrator. If you are sick or in poor health, you really cannot do your best on the exam. You can come back and take the test some other time.

VII. AT THE TEST

The day of the test is here and you have the test booklet in your hand. The temptation to get going is very strong. Caution! There is more to success than knowing the right answers. You must know how to identify your papers and understand variations in the type of short-answer question used in this particular examination. Follow these suggestions for maximum results from your efforts:

1) Cooperate with the monitor

The test administrator has a duty to create a situation in which you can be as much at ease as possible. He will give instructions, tell you when to begin, check to see that you are marking your answer sheet correctly, and so on. He is not there to guard you, although he will see that your competitors do not take unfair advantage. He wants to help you do your best.

2) Listen to all instructions

Don't jump the gun! Wait until you understand all directions. In most civil service tests you get more time than you need to answer the questions. So don't be in a hurry. Read each word of instructions until you clearly understand the meaning. Study the examples, listen to all announcements and follow directions. Ask questions if you do not understand what to do.

3) Identify your papers

Civil service exams are usually identified by number only. You will be assigned a number; you must not put your name on your test papers. Be sure to copy your number correctly. Since more than one exam may be given, copy your exact examination title.

4) Plan your time

Unless you are told that a test is a "speed" or "rate of work" test, speed itself is usually not important. Time enough to answer all the questions will be provided, but this does not mean that you have all day. An overall time limit has been set. Divide the total time (in minutes) by the number of questions to determine the approximate time you have for each question.

5) Do not linger over difficult questions

If you come across a difficult question, mark it with a paper clip (useful to have along) and come back to it when you have been through the booklet. One caution if you do this – be sure to skip a number on your answer sheet as well. Check often to be sure that you have not lost your place and that you are marking in the row numbered the same as the question you are answering.

6) Read the questions

Be sure you know what the question asks! Many capable people are unsuccessful because they failed to *read* the questions correctly.

7) Answer all questions

Unless you have been instructed that a penalty will be deducted for incorrect answers, it is better to guess than to omit a question.

8) Speed tests

It is often better NOT to guess on speed tests. It has been found that on timed tests people are tempted to spend the last few seconds before time is called in marking answers at random – without even reading them – in the hope of picking up a few extra points. To discourage this practice, the instructions may warn you that your score will be "corrected" for guessing. That is, a penalty will be applied. The incorrect answers will be deducted from the correct ones, or some other penalty formula will be used.

9) Review your answers

If you finish before time is called, go back to the questions you guessed or omitted to give them further thought. Review other answers if you have time.

10) Return your test materials

If you are ready to leave before others have finished or time is called, take ALL your materials to the monitor and leave quietly. Never take any test material with you. The monitor can discover whose papers are not complete, and taking a test booklet may be grounds for disqualification.

VIII. EXAMINATION TECHNIQUES

1) Read the general instructions carefully. These are usually printed on the first page of the exam booklet. As a rule, these instructions refer to the timing of the examination; the fact that you should not start work until the signal and must stop work at a signal, etc. If there are any *special* instructions, such as a choice of questions to be answered, make sure that you note this instruction carefully.

2) When you are ready to start work on the examination, that is as soon as the signal has been given, read the instructions to each question booklet, underline any key words or phrases, such as *least, best, outline, describe* and the like. In this way you will tend to answer as requested rather than discover on reviewing your paper that you *listed without describing*, that you selected the *worst* choice rather than the *best* choice, etc.

3) If the examination is of the objective or multiple-choice type – that is, each question will also give a series of possible answers: A, B, C or D, and you are called upon to select the best answer and write the letter next to that answer on your answer paper – it is advisable to start answering each question in turn. There may be anywhere from 50 to 100 such questions in the three or four hours allotted and you can see how much time would be taken if you read through all the questions before beginning to answer any. Furthermore, if you come across a question or group of questions which you know would be difficult to answer, it would undoubtedly affect your handling of all the other questions.

4) If the examination is of the essay type and contains but a few questions, it is a moot point as to whether you should read all the questions before starting to answer any one. Of course, if you are given a choice – say five out of seven and the like – then it is essential to read all the questions so you can eliminate the two that are most difficult. If, however, you are asked to answer all the questions, there may be danger in trying to answer the easiest one first because you may find that you will spend too much time on it. The best technique is to answer the first question, then proceed to the second, etc.

5) Time your answers. Before the exam begins, write down the time it started, then add the time allowed for the examination and write down the time it must be completed, then divide the time available somewhat as follows:
   - If 3-1/2 hours are allowed, that would be 210 minutes. If you have 80 objective-type questions, that would be an average of 2-1/2 minutes per question. Allow yourself no more than 2 minutes per question, or a total of 160 minutes, which will permit about 50 minutes to review.
   - If for the time allotment of 210 minutes there are 7 essay questions to answer, that would average about 30 minutes a question. Give yourself only 25 minutes per question so that you have about 35 minutes to review.

6) The most important instruction is to *read each question* and make sure you know what is wanted. The second most important instruction is to *time yourself properly* so that you answer every question. The third most important instruction is to *answer every question*. Guess if you have to but include something for each question. Remember that you will receive no credit for a blank and will probably receive some credit if you write something in answer to an essay question. If you guess a letter – say "B" for a multiple-choice question – you may have guessed right. If you leave a blank as an answer to a multiple-choice question, the examiners may respect your feelings but it will not add a point to your score. Some exams may penalize you for wrong answers, so in such cases *only*, you may not want to guess unless you have some basis for your answer.

7) Suggestions
   a. Objective-type questions
      1. Examine the question booklet for proper sequence of pages and questions
      2. Read all instructions carefully
      3. Skip any question which seems too difficult; return to it after all other questions have been answered
      4. Apportion your time properly; do not spend too much time on any single question or group of questions

5. Note and underline key words – *all, most, fewest, least, best, worst, same, opposite,* etc.
6. Pay particular attention to negatives
7. Note unusual option, e.g., unduly long, short, complex, different or similar in content to the body of the question
8. Observe the use of "hedging" words – *probably, may, most likely,* etc.
9. Make sure that your answer is put next to the same number as the question
10. Do not second-guess unless you have good reason to believe the second answer is definitely more correct
11. Cross out original answer if you decide another answer is more accurate; do not erase until you are ready to hand your paper in
12. Answer all questions; guess unless instructed otherwise
13. Leave time for review

b. Essay questions
1. Read each question carefully
2. Determine exactly what is wanted. Underline key words or phrases.
3. Decide on outline or paragraph answer
4. Include many different points and elements unless asked to develop any one or two points or elements
5. Show impartiality by giving pros and cons unless directed to select one side only
6. Make and write down any assumptions you find necessary to answer the questions
7. Watch your English, grammar, punctuation and choice of words
8. Time your answers; don't crowd material

8) Answering the essay question

Most essay questions can be answered by framing the specific response around several key words or ideas. Here are a few such key words or ideas:

M's: manpower, materials, methods, money, management
P's: purpose, program, policy, plan, procedure, practice, problems, pitfalls, personnel, public relations

a. Six basic steps in handling problems:
1. Preliminary plan and background development
2. Collect information, data and facts
3. Analyze and interpret information, data and facts
4. Analyze and develop solutions as well as make recommendations
5. Prepare report and sell recommendations
6. Install recommendations and follow up effectiveness

b. Pitfalls to avoid
1. *Taking things for granted* – A statement of the situation does not necessarily imply that each of the elements is necessarily true; for example, a complaint may be invalid and biased so that all that can be taken for granted is that a complaint has been registered

2. *Considering only one side of a situation* – Wherever possible, indicate several alternatives and then point out the reasons you selected the best one
3. *Failing to indicate follow up* – Whenever your answer indicates action on your part, make certain that you will take proper follow-up action to see how successful your recommendations, procedures or actions turn out to be
4. *Taking too long in answering any single question* – Remember to time your answers properly

IX. AFTER THE TEST

Scoring procedures differ in detail among civil service jurisdictions although the general principles are the same. Whether the papers are hand-scored or graded by machine we have described, they are nearly always graded by number. That is, the person who marks the paper knows only the number – never the name – of the applicant. Not until all the papers have been graded will they be matched with names. If other tests, such as training and experience or oral interview ratings have been given, scores will be combined. Different parts of the examination usually have different weights. For example, the written test might count 60 percent of the final grade, and a rating of training and experience 40 percent. In many jurisdictions, veterans will have a certain number of points added to their grades.

After the final grade has been determined, the names are placed in grade order and an eligible list is established. There are various methods for resolving ties between those who get the same final grade – probably the most common is to place first the name of the person whose application was received first. Job offers are made from the eligible list in the order the names appear on it. You will be notified of your grade and your rank as soon as all these computations have been made. This will be done as rapidly as possible.

People who are found to meet the requirements in the announcement are called "eligibles." Their names are put on a list of eligible candidates. An eligible's chances of getting a job depend on how high he stands on this list and how fast agencies are filling jobs from the list.

When a job is to be filled from a list of eligibles, the agency asks for the names of people on the list of eligibles for that job. When the civil service commission receives this request, it sends to the agency the names of the three people highest on this list. Or, if the job to be filled has specialized requirements, the office sends the agency the names of the top three persons who meet these requirements from the general list.

The appointing officer makes a choice from among the three people whose names were sent to him. If the selected person accepts the appointment, the names of the others are put back on the list to be considered for future openings.

That is the rule in hiring from all kinds of eligible lists, whether they are for typist, carpenter, chemist, or something else. For every vacancy, the appointing officer has his choice of any one of the top three eligibles on the list. This explains why the person whose name is on top of the list sometimes does not get an appointment when some of the persons lower on the list do. If the appointing officer chooses the second or third eligible, the No. 1 eligible does not get a job at once, but stays on the list until he is appointed or the list is terminated.

X. HOW TO PASS THE INTERVIEW TEST

The examination for which you applied requires an oral interview test. You have already taken the written test and you are now being called for the interview test – the final part of the formal examination.

You may think that it is not possible to prepare for an interview test and that there are no procedures to follow during an interview. Our purpose is to point out some things you can do in advance that will help you and some good rules to follow and pitfalls to avoid while you are being interviewed.

What is an interview supposed to test?

The written examination is designed to test the technical knowledge and competence of the candidate; the oral is designed to evaluate intangible qualities, not readily measured otherwise, and to establish a list showing the relative fitness of each candidate – as measured against his competitors – for the position sought. Scoring is not on the basis of "right" and "wrong," but on a sliding scale of values ranging from "not passable" to "outstanding." As a matter of fact, it is possible to achieve a relatively low score without a single "incorrect" answer because of evident weakness in the qualities being measured.

Occasionally, an examination may consist entirely of an oral test – either an individual or a group oral. In such cases, information is sought concerning the technical knowledges and abilities of the candidate, since there has been no written examination for this purpose. More commonly, however, an oral test is used to supplement a written examination.

Who conducts interviews?

The composition of oral boards varies among different jurisdictions. In nearly all, a representative of the personnel department serves as chairman. One of the members of the board may be a representative of the department in which the candidate would work. In some cases, "outside experts" are used, and, frequently, a businessman or some other representative of the general public is asked to serve. Labor and management or other special groups may be represented. The aim is to secure the services of experts in the appropriate field.

However the board is composed, it is a good idea (and not at all improper or unethical) to ascertain in advance of the interview who the members are and what groups they represent. When you are introduced to them, you will have some idea of their backgrounds and interests, and at least you will not stutter and stammer over their names.

What should be done before the interview?

While knowledge about the board members is useful and takes some of the surprise element out of the interview, there is other preparation which is more substantive. It *is* possible to prepare for an oral interview – in several ways:

1) Keep a copy of your application and review it carefully before the interview

This may be the only document before the oral board, and the starting point of the interview. Know what education and experience you have listed there, and the sequence and dates of all of it. Sometimes the board will ask you to review the highlights of your experience for them; you should not have to hem and haw doing it.

2) Study the class specification and the examination announcement

Usually, the oral board has one or both of these to guide them. The qualities, characteristics or knowledges required by the position sought are stated in these documents. They offer valuable clues as to the nature of the oral interview. For example, if the job involves supervisory responsibilities, the announcement will usually indicate that knowledge of modern supervisory methods and the qualifications of the candidate as a supervisor will be tested. If so, you can expect such questions, frequently in the form of a hypothetical situation which you are expected to solve. NEVER go into an oral without knowledge of the duties and responsibilities of the job you seek.

3) Think through each qualification required

Try to visualize the kind of questions you would ask if you were a board member. How well could you answer them? Try especially to appraise your own knowledge and background in each area, *measured against the job sought*, and identify any areas in which you are weak. Be critical and realistic – do not flatter yourself.

4) Do some general reading in areas in which you feel you may be weak

For example, if the job involves supervision and your past experience has NOT, some general reading in supervisory methods and practices, particularly in the field of human relations, might be useful. Do NOT study agency procedures or detailed manuals. The oral board will be testing your understanding and capacity, not your memory.

5) Get a good night's sleep and watch your general health and mental attitude

You will want a clear head at the interview. Take care of a cold or any other minor ailment, and of course, no hangovers.

What should be done on the day of the interview?

Now comes the day of the interview itself. Give yourself plenty of time to get there. Plan to arrive somewhat ahead of the scheduled time, particularly if your appointment is in the fore part of the day. If a previous candidate fails to appear, the board might be ready for you a bit early. By early afternoon an oral board is almost invariably behind schedule if there are many candidates, and you may have to wait. Take along a book or magazine to read, or your application to review, but leave any extraneous material in the waiting room when you go in for your interview. In any event, relax and compose yourself.

The matter of dress is important. The board is forming impressions about you – from your experience, your manners, your attitude, and your appearance. Give your personal appearance careful attention. Dress your best, but not your flashiest. Choose conservative, appropriate clothing, and be sure it is immaculate. This is a business interview, and your appearance should indicate that you regard it as such. Besides, being well groomed and properly dressed will help boost your confidence.

Sooner or later, someone will call your name and escort you into the interview room. *This is it.* From here on you are on your own. It is too late for any more preparation. But remember, you asked for this opportunity to prove your fitness, and you are here because your request was granted.

What happens when you go in?

The usual sequence of events will be as follows: The clerk (who is often the board stenographer) will introduce you to the chairman of the oral board, who will introduce you to the other members of the board. Acknowledge the introductions before you sit down. Do not be surprised if you find a microphone facing you or a stenotypist sitting by. Oral interviews are usually recorded in the event of an appeal or other review.

Usually the chairman of the board will open the interview by reviewing the highlights of your education and work experience from your application – primarily for the benefit of the other members of the board, as well as to get the material into the record. Do not interrupt or comment unless there is an error or significant misinterpretation; if that is the case, do not hesitate. But do not quibble about insignificant matters. Also, he will usually ask you some question about your education, experience or your present job – partly to get you to start talking and to establish the interviewing "rapport." He may start the actual questioning, or turn it over to one of the other members. Frequently, each member undertakes the questioning on a particular area, one in which he is perhaps most competent, so you can expect each member to participate in the examination. Because time is limited, you may also expect some rather abrupt switches in the direction the questioning takes, so do not be upset by it. Normally, a board member will not pursue a single line of questioning unless he discovers a particular strength or weakness.

After each member has participated, the chairman will usually ask whether any member has any further questions, then will ask you if you have anything you wish to add. Unless you are expecting this question, it may floor you. Worse, it may start you off on an extended, extemporaneous speech. The board is not usually seeking more information. The question is principally to offer you a last opportunity to present further qualifications or to indicate that you have nothing to add. So, if you feel that a significant qualification or characteristic has been overlooked, it is proper to point it out in a sentence or so. Do not compliment the board on the thoroughness of their examination – they have been sketchy, and you know it. If you wish, merely say, "No thank you, I have nothing further to add." This is a point where you can "talk yourself out" of a good impression or fail to present an important bit of information. Remember, *you close the interview yourself.*

The chairman will then say, "That is all, Mr. ______, thank you." Do not be startled; the interview is over, and quicker than you think. Thank him, gather your belongings and take your leave. Save your sigh of relief for the other side of the door.

How to put your best foot forward

Throughout this entire process, you may feel that the board individually and collectively is trying to pierce your defenses, seek out your hidden weaknesses and embarrass and confuse you. Actually, this is not true. They are obliged to make an appraisal of your qualifications for the job you are seeking, and they want to see you in your best light. Remember, they must interview all candidates and a non-cooperative candidate may become a failure in spite of their best efforts to bring out his qualifications. Here are 15 suggestions that will help you:

1) Be natural – Keep your attitude confident, not cocky

If you are not confident that you can do the job, do not expect the board to be. Do not apologize for your weaknesses, try to bring out your strong points. The board is interested in a positive, not negative, presentation. Cockiness will antagonize any board member and make him wonder if you are covering up a weakness by a false show of strength.

2) Get comfortable, but don't lounge or sprawl

Sit erectly but not stiffly. A careless posture may lead the board to conclude that you are careless in other things, or at least that you are not impressed by the importance of the occasion. Either conclusion is natural, even if incorrect. Do not fuss with your clothing, a pencil or an ashtray. Your hands may occasionally be useful to emphasize a point; do not let them become a point of distraction.

3) Do not wisecrack or make small talk

This is a serious situation, and your attitude should show that you consider it as such. Further, the time of the board is limited – they do not want to waste it, and neither should you.

4) Do not exaggerate your experience or abilities

In the first place, from information in the application or other interviews and sources, the board may know more about you than you think. Secondly, you probably will not get away with it. An experienced board is rather adept at spotting such a situation, so do not take the chance.

5) If you know a board member, do not make a point of it, yet do not hide it

Certainly you are not fooling him, and probably not the other members of the board. Do not try to take advantage of your acquaintanceship – it will probably do you little good.

6) Do not dominate the interview

Let the board do that. They will give you the clues – do not assume that you have to do all the talking. Realize that the board has a number of questions to ask you, and do not try to take up all the interview time by showing off your extensive knowledge of the answer to the first one.

7) Be attentive

You only have 20 minutes or so, and you should keep your attention at its sharpest throughout. When a member is addressing a problem or question to you, give him your undivided attention. Address your reply principally to him, but do not exclude the other board members.

8) Do not interrupt

A board member may be stating a problem for you to analyze. He will ask you a question when the time comes. Let him state the problem, and wait for the question.

9) Make sure you understand the question

Do not try to answer until you are sure what the question is. If it is not clear, restate it in your own words or ask the board member to clarify it for you. However, do not haggle about minor elements.

10) Reply promptly but not hastily

A common entry on oral board rating sheets is "candidate responded readily," or "candidate hesitated in replies." Respond as promptly and quickly as you can, but do not jump to a hasty, ill-considered answer.

11) Do not be peremptory in your answers

A brief answer is proper – but do not fire your answer back. That is a losing game from your point of view. The board member can probably ask questions much faster than you can answer them.

12) Do not try to create the answer you think the board member wants

He is interested in what kind of mind you have and how it works – not in playing games. Furthermore, he can usually spot this practice and will actually grade you down on it.

13) Do not switch sides in your reply merely to agree with a board member

Frequently, a member will take a contrary position merely to draw you out and to see if you are willing and able to defend your point of view. Do not start a debate, yet do not surrender a good position. If a position is worth taking, it is worth defending.

14) Do not be afraid to admit an error in judgment if you are shown to be wrong

The board knows that you are forced to reply without any opportunity for careful consideration. Your answer may be demonstrably wrong. If so, admit it and get on with the interview.

15) Do not dwell at length on your present job

The opening question may relate to your present assignment. Answer the question but do not go into an extended discussion. You are being examined for a *new* job, not your present one. As a matter of fact, try to phrase ALL your answers in terms of the job for which you are being examined.

Basis of Rating

Probably you will forget most of these "do's" and "don'ts" when you walk into the oral interview room. Even remembering them all will not ensure you a passing grade. Perhaps you did not have the qualifications in the first place. But remembering them will help you to put your best foot forward, without treading on the toes of the board members.

Rumor and popular opinion to the contrary notwithstanding, an oral board wants you to make the best appearance possible. They know you are under pressure – but they also want to see how you respond to it as a guide to what your reaction would be under the pressures of the job you seek. They will be influenced by the degree of poise you display, the personal traits you show and the manner in which you respond.

ABOUT THIS BOOK

This book contains tests divided into Examination Sections. Go through each test, answering every question in the margin. We have also attached a sample answer sheet at the back of the book that can be removed and used. At the end of each test look at the answer key and check your answers. On the ones you got wrong, look at the right answer choice and learn. Do not fill in the answers first. Do not memorize the questions and answers, but understand the answer and principles involved. On your test, the questions will likely be different from the samples. Questions are changed and new ones added. If you understand these past questions you should have success with any changes that arise. Tests may consist of several types of questions. We have additional books on each subject should more study be advisable or necessary for you. Finally, the more you study, the better prepared you will be. This book is intended to be the last thing you study before you walk into the examination room. Prior study of relevant texts is also recommended. NLC publishes some of these in our Fundamental Series. Knowledge and good sense are important factors in passing your exam. Good luck also helps. So now study this Passbook, absorb the material contained within and take that knowledge into the examination. Then do your best to pass that exam.

EXAMINATION SECTION

EXAMINATION SECTION
TEST 1

DIRECTIONS: Each question or incomplete statement is followed by several suggested answers or completions. Select the one that BEST answers the question or completes the statement. *PRINT THE LETTER OF THE CORRECT ANSWER IN THE SPACE AT THE RIGHT.*

1. You have recently been assigned to a new office and are expected to supervise six clerks. 1.____
All of the following would be good introductory steps to take EXCEPT

   A. giving a clear presentation of yourself to the clerks, including a short summary of your recent work experience
   B. initiating informal discussions with each clerk concerning his work
   C. making a general survey of all the functions which each clerk has been performing
   D. making a list of the duties each clerk is required to perform and giving it to the clerk

2. Your supervisor has advised you that a specific aspect of a job is being done incorrectly and you acknowledge the mistake. 2.____
Of the following, the MOST efficient way of dealing with this situation is to

   A. call a meeting of the clerks who are performing this particular function and explain the correct method
   B. assume the blame and correct the errors as they are given to you
   C. speak with each clerk individually and carefully show each one the proper method
   D. distribute a set of written instructions covering all clerical procedures to the employees doing that particular job

3. A new department regulation calls for a change in a particular method of processing new applications. Two clerks have complained to you that the new method is more time-consuming, and they prefer to do it the original way. 3.____
Of the following, what is the MOST advisable thing to do?

   A. Discuss the situation with them and attempt to determine whether they are utilizing the method properly.
   B. Discuss the advantages of both methods with them and let them use the one that is more practical.
   C. Firmly instruct the clerks to proceed with the new method since it is not up to them to refute department policy.
   D. Tell them to survey the opinions of the other clerks on this matter and inform you of the results.

4. A member of the clerical staff has recently begun reporting late for work rather regularly. On each occasion, the individual presented an excuse, but the latenesses continue. 4.____
Of the following, the MOST advisable action for her supervisor to take is to

   A. have a staff meeting and stress the importance of being on time for work, without singling out the specific individual
   B. put a notice on the departmental office bulletin board, specifying and stressing that lateness can not be tolerated

C. talk privately with the individual to determine whether there are any unusual circumstances that might be causing the lateness
D. send the individual a memorandum clearly indicating that continual lateness will result in disciplinary action

5. Assume that, as the supervisor of a unit, you have been asked to prepare a vacation schedule for your subordinate employees. The employees have had different lengths of service. Some of them have already submitted requests for certain weeks. 5.____
Of the following, which factor would be LEAST important in setting up this schedule?

A. Your opinion of each employee's past work performance
B. Each employee's preference for a vacation period
C. The amount of work the unit is expected to accomplish during the vacation period
D. The number of employees who have requested to go on vacation at the same time

6. Your superior finds that he must leave the office one day before he has had time to check and sign the day's correspondence. He asks you to proofread the letters, have corrections made where necessary, and then sign his name. You have never signed his name before. 6.____
Of the following, the BEST thing for you to do is to

A. sign your superior's name in full, making it look as much like his handwriting as possible
B. sign your superior's name and your own name in full as proof that you signed for him
C. sign your superior's name in full and add your initials to show that the signature is not his own
D. politely refuse to sign his name because it is forgery

7. The head of your office sometimes makes handwritten notations on original letters which he receives and requests that you mail the letters back to the sender. Of the following, the BEST action for you to take FIRST is to 7.____

A. request that this practice be stopped because it does not provide for a record in the files
B. request that this practice be stopped because it is not the customary way to respond to letters
C. photocopy the letters so that there are copies for the file and then send the letters out
D. ask the head of your office if he wants you to keep any record of the letters

8. The main function of most agency administrative offices is *information management.* Information that is received by an administrative office may be classified as active (information which requires the recipient to take some action) or passive (information which does not require action). 8.____
Which one of the following items received must clearly be treated as ACTIVE information?
A(n)

A. confirmation of payment
B. press release concerning an agency event
C. advertisement for a new restaurant opening near the agency
D. request for a student transcript

9. Which of the following statements about the use of the photocopy process is CORRECT? 9.____

A. It is difficult to use.
B. It can be used to reproduce color.
C. It does not print well on colored paper.
D. Once source documents have been used, they cannot be used again.

10. In order to get the BEST estimate of how long a repetitive office procedure should take, a supervisor should find out how 10.____

A. long it takes her best worker to do the procedure once on a typical day
B. long it takes her best and worst workers to do the procedure once on a typical day
C. much time her best worker spends on the procedure during a typical week and the total number of times the worker executes the procedure during the same week
D. much time all her subordinates spend on the procedure during a typical week and the total number of times the procedure was executed during the same week by all employees

11. Of the following, the MOST suitable and appropriate way to make 250 copies of a particular form is to 11.____

A. print all 250 copies on the office computer
B. delegate the work to someone else
C. reproduce it on a photocopying machine
D. use an offset printing process

Questions 12-18.

DIRECTIONS: Questions 12 through 18 are to be answered on the basis of the extracts shown below from Federal withholding tables. These tables indicate the amounts which must be withheld from the employee's salary by his employer for Federal income tax and for social security. They are based on weekly earnings.

INCOME TAX WITHHOLDING TABLE

The wages are -		And the number of withholding exemptions claimed is-					
At least	But less than	0	1	2	3	4	5
		The amount of income tax to be withheld shall be -					
$200	$205	$14.10	$11.80	$ 9.50	$ 7.20	$ 4.90	$2.80
205	210	14.90	12.60	10.30	8.00	5.70	3.50
210	215	15.70	13.40	11.10	8.80	6.50	4.20
215	220	16.50	14.20	11.90	9.60	7.30	5.00
220	225	17.30	15.00	12.70	10.40	8.10	5.80
225	230	18.10	15.80	13.50	11.20	8.90	6.60
230	235	18.90	16.60	14.30	12.00	9.70	7.40
235	240	19.70	17.40	15.10	12.80	10.50	8.20
240	245	20.50	18.20	15.90	13.60	11.30	9.00
245	250	21.30	19.00	16.70	14.40	12.10	9.80

SOCIAL SECURITY EMPLOYEE TAX TABLE

Wages		Tax to be withheld	Wages		Tax to be withheld
At least	But less than		At least	But less than	
$202.79	$202.99	$15.35	$229.72	$229.91	$16.75
202.99	203.18	15.36	229.91	230.10	16.76
203.18	203.37	15.37	230.10	230.29	16.77
203.37	203.56	15.38	230.29	230.49	16.78
203.56	203.75	15.39	230.49	230.68	16.79
203.75	203.95	15.40	230.68	230.87	16.80
203.95	204.14	15.41	230.87	231.06	16.81
204.14	204.33	15.42	231.06	231.25	16.82
204.33	204.52	15.43	231.25	231.45	16.83
204.52	204.72	15.44	231.45	231.64	16.84

Wages		Tax to be withheld	Wages		Tax to be withheld
At least	But less than		At least	But less than	
$222.02	$222.22	$16.35	$234.52	$234.72	$17.00
222.22	222.41	16.36	234.72	234.91	17.01
222.41	222.60	16.37	234.91	235.10	17.02
222.60	222.79	16.38	235.10	235.29	17.03
222.79	222.99	16.39	235.29	235.49	17.04
222.99	223.18	16.40	235.49	235.68	17.05
223.18	223.37	16.41	235.68	235.87	17.06
223.37	223.56	16.42	235.87	236.06	17.07
223.56	223.75	16.43	236.06	236.25	17.08
223.75	223.95	16.44	236.25	236.45	17.09

12. Dave Andes has wages of $242.75 for one week. He has claimed three withholding exemptions. 12.____
What is the Federal income tax which should be withheld?

A. $13.60 B. $15.90 C. $18.20 D. $20.50

13. Mary Hodes has wages of $229.95 for one week. 13.____
What is the Social Security tax which should be withheld?

A. $16.75 B. $16.76 C. $16.77 D. $16.78

14. Joe Jones had wages of $235.63 for one week. He has claimed two withholding exemptions. 14.____
What is the Federal income tax which should be withheld?

A. $12.80 B. $14.30 C. $15.10 D. $17.40

15. Tom Stein had wages of $203.95 for one week. What is the Social Security tax which should be withheld? 15.____

A. $15.40 B. $15.41 C. $16.05 D. $16.06

16. Robert Helman had wages of $222.80 for one week. He has claimed one withholding exemption. 16.____
If only Federal income tax and Social Security tax were deducted from his earnings for the same week, how much *take-home* pay should he have for the week?

A. $191.41 B. $193.96 C. $194.12 D. $195.65

17. Audrey Stein has wages of $203.00 for one week. She claimed no withholding exemptions. 17.____
If only Federal income tax and Social Security tax were deducted from her earnings for the same week, how much *take-home* pay should she have for the week?

A. $171.84 B. $172.34 C. $173.54 D. $175.84

18. Anthony Covallo, who worked 28 hours in the past week, has a regular hourly rate of $7.25 per hour and earns a premium of time and a half for hours over 40. He has claimed four withholding exemptions. 18.____
After Social Security tax and Federal income tax are deducted from his wages for the past week, how much pay does he have left?

A. $180.98 B. $181.13 C. $182.29 D. $182.74

19. In judging the adequacy of a standard office form, which of the following is LEAST important? 19.____
_______ of the form.

A. Date B. Legibility C. Size D. Design

20. Clear and accurate telephone messages should be taken for employees who are out of the office. 20.____
Which of the following is of LEAST importance when taking a telephone message?

A. Name of the person called
B. Name of the caller

C. Details of the message
D. Time of the call

21. Suppose that all office supplies are kept in a centrally located cabinet in the office. Of the following, which is usually the BEST policy to adhere to for distribution of supplies? 21.____

A. Permit employees to stock up on all supplies to avoid frequent trips to the cabinet.
B. Assign one employee to be in charge of distributing all supplies to other employees at frequent intervals.
C. Inform employees that supplies should be taken in large quantities and only when needed.
D. Keep cabinet closed and instruct employees that they must check with you before taking supplies.

Questions 22-25.

DIRECTIONS: Questions 22 through 25 are to be answered SOLELY on the basis of the following passage.

Use of the systems and procedures approach to office management is revolutionizing the supervision of office work. This approach views an enterprise as an entity which seeks to fulfill definite objectives. Systems and procedures help to organize repetitive work into a routine, thus reducing the amount of decision-making required for its accomplishment. As a result, employees are guided in their efforts and perform only necessary work. Supervisors are relieved of any details of execution and are free to attend to more important work. Establishing work guides which require that identical tasks be performed the same way each, time permits standardization of forms, machine operations, work methods, and controls. This approach also reduces the probability of errors. Any error committed is usually discovered quickly because the incorrect work does not meet the requirement of the work guides. Errors are also reduced through work specialization which allows each employee to become thoroughly proficient in a particular type of work. Such proficiency also tends to improve the morale of the employees.

22. Of the following, which one BEST expresses the main theme of the above passage? The 22.____

A. advantages and disadvantages of the systems and procedures approach to office management
B. effectiveness of the systems and procedures approach to office management in developing skills
C. systems and procedures approach to office management as it relates to office costs
D. advantages of the systems and procedures approach to office management for supervisors and office workers

23. Work guides are LEAST likely to be used when 23.____

A. standardized forms are used
B. a particular office task is distinct and different from all others
C. identical tasks are to be performed in identical ways
D. similar work methods are expected from each employee

24. According to the above passage, when an employee makes a work error, it USUALLY 24.____

A. is quickly corrected by the supervisor
B. necessitates a change in the work guides
C. can be detected quickly if work guides are in use
D. increases the probability of further errors by that employee

25. The above passage states that the accuracy of an employee's work is INCREASED by 25.____

A. using the work specialization approach
B. employing a probability sample
C. requiring him to shift at one time into different types of tasks
D. having his supervisor check each detail of work execution

KEY (CORRECT ANSWERS)

1.	D	11.	C
2.	A	12.	A
3.	A	13.	B
4.	C	14.	C
5.	A	15.	B
6.	C	16.	A
7.	D	17.	C
8.	D	18.	D
9.	B	19.	A
10.	D	20.	D

21. B
22. D
23. B
24. C
25. A

TEST 2

DIRECTIONS: Each question or incomplete statement is followed by several suggested answers or completions. Select the one that BEST answers the question or completes the statement. *PRINT THE LETTER OF THE CORRECT ANSWER IN THE SPACE AT THE RIGHT.*

1. A certain supervisor often holds group meetings with subordinates to discuss the goals of the unit and manpower requirements for meeting objectives. 1.___
For the supervisor to hold such meetings is a

   A. *good* practice because it will aid both the supervisor and subordinates in planning and completing the unit's work
   B. *good* practice because it will prevent future problems from interfering with the unit's objectives
   C. *poor* practice because the supervisor has the sole responsibility for meeting objectives and should make manpower decisions without any advice
   D. *poor* practice because the subordinates will be allowed to set their own work quotas

2. Assume that you are a supervisor who has been asked to evaluate the work of a clerk who was transferred to your unit about six months ago. 2.___
Which one of the following, by itself, provides the BEST basis for making such an evaluation?

   A. Ask the clerk's former supervisor about the employee's previous work.
   B. Ask the clerk's co-workers for their opinions of the employee's work.
   C. Evaluate the quantity and quality of the employee's work over the six-month period.
   D. Observe the employee's performance from time to time during the next week and base your evaluation on these observations.

3. Which of the following would be the MOST desirable way for a supervisor to help improve the job performance of a particular subordinate? 3.___

   A. Criticize the employee's performance in front of other employees.
   B. Privately warn the employee that failure to meet work standards may lead to dismissal.
   C. Hold a meeting with this employee and other subordinates in which the need to improve the unit's performance is stressed.
   D. Meet privately with the employee and discuss both positive and negative aspects of the employee's work

4. Suppose that your office has a limited supply of a pamphlet which people may read in your office when they seek certain information, but another office in your building is supposed to have a large supply available for distribution to the public. 4.___
Which of the following would be the BEST thing for you to do when someone states that he has not been able to obtain one of these pamphlets?

   A. Tell him that he misunderstood the directions that other employees have given him and carefully direct him to the other office.
   B. Ask whether he has visited the other office and requested a copy from them.
   C. Let him take one of your office's copies of the pamphlet and then call the other office and ask why they have run out of copies for distribution.

D. Tell him that your office does its best to keep the public informed but that this might not be true of other offices.

5. On Monday, a clerk made many errors in completing a new daily record form. The supervisor explained the errors and had the clerk correct the form. On Tuesday, the clerk made fewer errors. Because he was very busy, the supervisor did not point out the errors to the clerk but corrected the errors himself. On Wednesday, the clerk made the same number of errors as on Tuesday. The supervisor reprimanded the clerk for making so many errors. 5.____
The supervisor's handling of this situation on Wednesday may be considered poor MAINLY because the

A. clerk was not given enough time to complete each form properly
B. supervisor should not have expected improvement without further training
C. clerk was obviously incapable of completing the form
D. supervisor should have continued to correct the errors himself

Questions 6-8.

DIRECTIONS: Questions 6 through 8 are to be answered SOLELY on the basis of the information contained in the following passage.

When using words like company, association, *council, committee, and board in place of the full official name, the writer should not capitalize these short forms unless he intends them to invoke the full force of the institution's authority. In legal contracts, in minutes, or in formal correspondence where one is speaking formally and officially on behalf of the company, the term "Company" is usually capitalized, but in ordinary usage, where it is not essential to load the short form with this significance, capitalization would be excessive. (Example: The company will have many good openings for graduates this June.)*

The treatment recommended for short forms of place names is essentially the same as that recommended for short forms of organizational names. In general, we capitalize the full form but not the short form. If Park Avenue is referred to in one sentence, then "the avenue" is sufficient in subsequent references. The same is true with words like building, hotel, station, and airport, which are capitalized when part of a proper name (Pan Am Building, Hotel Plaza, Union Station, O'Hare Airport) but are simply lower-cased when replacing these specific names.

6. The above passage states that USUALLY the short forms of names of organizations 6.____

A. and places should not be capitalized
B. and places should be capitalized
C. should not be capitalized, but the short forms of names of places should be capitalized
D. should be capitalized, but the short forms of names of places should not be capitalized

7. The above passage states that in legal contracts, in minutes, and in formal correspondence, the short forms of names of organizations should 7.____

A. usually not be capitalized
B. usually be capitalized
C. usually not be used
D. never be used

8. It can be INFERRED from the above passage that decisions regarding when to capitalize certain words 8.___

A. should be left to the discretion of the writer
B. should be based on generally accepted rules
C. depend on the total number of words capitalized
D. are of minor importance

9. The Central Terminal and the Gardens Terminal are located on Glover Street. 9.___
In ordinary usage, if this sentence were to be followed by the sentence in the choices below, which form of the sentence would be CORRECT?

A. Both Terminals are situated on the same street.
B. Both terminals are situated on the same Street.
C. Both terminals are situated on the same street.
D. Both Terminals are situated on the same Street.

10. A stylus is a(n) 10.___

A. implement for writing containing a cylinder of graphite
B. implement for writing with ink or a similar fluid
C. pointed implement used to write
D. stick of colored wax used for writing

11. As a supervisor, you have the responsibility of teaching new employees the functions and procedures of your office after their orientation by the personnel office. 11.___
Of the following, the BEST way to begin such instruction is to

A. advise the new employee of the benefits and services available to him, over and above his salary
B. discuss the negative aspects of the departmental procedures and indicate methods available to overcome them
C. assist the new employee in understanding the general purpose of the office procedures and how they fit in with the overall operation
D. give a detailed briefing of the operations of your office, its functions and procedures

12. Assume that you are the supervisor of a clerical unit. One of the duties of the employees in your unit is to conduct a brief interview with persons using the services of your agency for the first time. The purpose of the interview is to get general background information in order to best direct them to the appropriate division. 12.___
A clerk comes to your office and says that a prospective client has just called her some rather unpleasant names, accused her of being nosey and meddlesome, and has stated emphatically that she refuses to talk with an *underling,* meaning the clerk. The young woman is almost in tears. Of the following, what is the FIRST action you should take?

A. Immediately call the agency's protection officer, have him advise the client of the regulations, and tell her that she will be removed if she is not more polite.
B. Calm the clerk, introduce yourself to the client, and quietly discuss the agency's services, regulations, and informational needs, and request that she complete the interview with the clerk.

C. Calm the clerk, have her return and firmly advise the client of the agency's rules concerning the need for this first interview.
D. Introduce yourself to the client and advise her that without an apology to the clerk and completion of the interview, she will not be given any service.

13. A recent high school graduate has just been assigned to the unit which you supervise. Which of the following would be the LEAST desirable technique to use with this employee? 13.____

A. At any one time, give the new employee only as much detail about the job as the employee can absorb.
B. Always tell the new employee the correct procedure, then demonstrate how it is accomplished.
C. Assign the employee the same quantity and type of work that the other employees are doing to see if the employee can handle the job.
D. Assume the employee is tense and be prepared to repeat procedures and descriptions.

14. Assume that you supervise a work unit of several employees. Which of the following is LEAST essential in assuring that the goals which you set for the unit are achieved? 14.____

A. Establishing objectives and standards for the staff
B. Providing justification for disciplinary action
C. Measuring performance or progress of individuals against standards
D. Taking corrective action where performance is less than expected

15. One of the clerks you supervise is often reluctant to accept assignments and usually complains about the amount of work expected, although the other clerks with the same assignments and workload seem quite happy.
Of the following, the MOST accurate assumption that you can make about this clerk is that she 15.____

A. will require additional observation and help
B. will eventually have to be discharged or transferred
C. is incompetent
D. is overworked

Questions 16-21.

DIRECTIONS: Questions 16 through 21 are to be answered SOLELY on the basis of the airline timetable and the information appearing on the last page of this test.

Fact Situation:

An administrator wants you to purchase airline tickets for him so that he can attend a meeting being held in Chicago on Monday. He must leave from LaGuardia Airport in New York on Monday morning as late as possible but with arrival in Chicago no later than 9:00 A.M. He wishes to fly coach/economy class both ways. The meeting is due to end at 5:30 P.M., and he wishes to obtain the first plane after 6:45 P.M. going back to LaGuardia Airport. If all these requirements have been met, he would, if possible, also like to fly to and leave from Midway Airport in Chicago and go non-stop both ways.

16. You should obtain a ticket for the administrator from New York to Chicago on flight number 16.___

A. 483 B. 201 C. 277 D. 539

17. You should obtain a ticket for the administrator from Chicago to New York on flight number 17.___

A. 588 B. 692 C. 268 D. 334

18. The administrator decides to take limousines to and from both airports. 18.___
If the limousine charge in Chicago is $52.50. and there is no reduced rate for a round-trip flight, what is the cost of the administrator's round-trip air fare PLUS limousine service?

A. $827.50 B. $931.00 C. $963.00 D. $967.00

19. The administrator asked you whether he would be able to get breakfast on his flight to Chicago or whether he should go to the airport early and eat there before boarding the plane. He prefers to eat on the plane. 19.___
Of the following, the BEST reply to make is:

A. I will have to telephone the airport to find out
B. You should eat at the airport
C. A meal is served on the plane
D. Only certain passengers get a meal on the plane

20. Of the following requests of the administrator concerning his travel arrangements, which one is IMPOSSIBLE to meet? 20.___

A. Chicago arrival no later than 9 A.M.
B. New York departure from LaGuardia Airport
C. Non-stop flights both ways
D. Chicago departure from Midway Airport

21. Suppose that it is necessary to take a first-class seat on the trip to Chicago although you have no problem reserving a coach/economy seat on the return trip. 21.___
If there is no reduction in fare for round-trip flights, how much MORE will this trip cost than round-trip coach/ economy?

A. $209 B. $236 C. $318 D. $636

22. Ms. X, a clerk under your supervision, has been working in the unit for a few weeks. Some of the other employees have complained to you that Ms. X has an annoying habit of constantly tapping her feet on the floor and it disturbs their work. 22.___
The BEST thing for you to do is to

A. ignore the complaints because the employees should be concerned only with their own habits
B. speak with Ms. X privately and discuss the situation with her
C. make a general announcement that employees should control their nervous habits
D. observe Ms. X for a few weeks to see if the employees are correct, and then take action

23. Suppose you answer a telephone call from someone who states that he is a friend of one of your co-workers and needs the employee's new address in order to send an invitation. Your co-worker is on vacation but you know her address. Which of the following is the BEST action for you to take? 23.____

A. Give the caller the address but ask the caller not to mention that you are the one who gave it out.
B. Give the caller the address and leave a note for your co-worker stating what you did.
C. Tell the caller you do not know the address but will give the employee's phone number if that will help.
D. Offer to take his name and address and have your co-worker contact him.

24. Assume that you receive a telephone call in which the caller requests information which you know is posted in the office next to yours. You start to tell the caller you will transfer her call to the right office, but she interrupts you and says she has been transferred from office to office and is tired of getting a *run-around*. Of the following, the BEST thing for you to do is to 24.____

A. give the caller the phone number of the office next to yours and quickly end the conversation
B. give her the phone number of the office next to yours and tell her you will try to transfer her call
C. ask her if she wants to hold on while you get the information for her
D. tell the caller that she could have avoided the *run-around* by asking for the right office, and suggest that she come in person

25. Assume that your unit processes confidential forms which are submitted by persons seeking financial assistance. An individual comes to your office, gives you his name, and states that he would like to look over a form which he sent in about a week ago because he believes he omitted some important information. Of the following, the BEST thing for you to do FIRST is to 25.____

A. locate the proper form
B. call the individual's home telephone number to verify his identity
C. ask the individual if he has proof of his identity
D. call the security office

KEY (CORRECT ANSWERS)

1. A
2. C
3. D
4. B
5. B
6. A
7. B
8. B
9. C
10. C
11. C
12. B
13. C
14. B
15. A
16. A
17. D
18. B
19. C
20. D
21. C
22. B
23. D
24. C
25. C

EXAMINATION SECTION
TEST 1

DIRECTIONS: Each question or incomplete statement is followed by several suggested answers or completions. Select the one that BEST answers the question or completes the statement. *PRINT THE LETTER OF THE CORRECT ANSWER IN THE SPACE AT THE RIGHT.*

1. Suppose that you are requested to transmit to the stenographers in your bureau an order curtailing certain privileges that they have been enjoying. You anticipate that your staff may resent curtailment of such privileges. Of the following, the BEST action for you to take is to 1.____

   A. impress upon your staff that an order is an order and must be obeyed
   B. attempt to explain to your staff the probable reasons for curtailing their privileges
   C. excuse the curtailment of privileges by saying that the welfare of the staff was evidently not considered
   D. warn your staff that violation of an order may be considered sufficient cause for immediate dismissal

2. The supervisor should set a good example. 2.____
   Of the following, the CHIEF implication of the above statement is that the supervisor should

   A. behave as he expects his workers to behave
   B. know as much about the work as his workers do
   C. keep his workers informed of what he is doing
   D. keep ahead of his workers

3. Of the following, the LEAST desirable procedure for the competent supervisor to follow is to 3.____

   A. organize his work before taking responsibility for helping others with theirs
   B. avoid schedules and routines when he is busy
   C. be flexible in planning and carrying out his responsibilities
   D. secure the support of his staff in organizing the total job of the unit

4. Evaluation helps the worker by increasing his security. 4.____
   Of the following, the BEST justification for this statement is that

   A. security and growth depend upon knowledge by the worker of the agency's evaluation
   B. knowledge of his evaluation by agency and supervisor will stimulate the worker to better performance
   C. evaluation enables the supervisor and worker to determine the reasons for the worker's strengths and weaknesses
   D. the supervisor and worker together can usually recognize and deal with any worker's insecurity

5. A supervisor may encourage his subordinates to make suggestions by 5.____

   A. keeping a record of the number of suggestions an employee makes
   B. providing a suggestion box

C. outlining a list of possible suggestions
D. giving credit to a subordinate whose suggestion has been accepted and used

6. If you were required to give service ratings to employees under your supervision, you should consider as MOST important during the current period the 6.____

A. personal characteristics and salary and grade of an employee
B. length of service and the volume of work performed
C. previous service rating given him
D. personal characteristics and the quality of work of an employee

7. A supervisor must consider many factors in evaluating a worker whom he has supervised for a considerable time. In evaluating the capacity of such a worker to use independent judgment, the one of the following to which the supervisor should generally give MOST consideration is the worker's 7.____

A. capacity to establish good relationships with people (clients and colleagues)
B. educational background
C. emotional stability
D. the quality and judgment shown by the investigator in previous work situations known to the supervisor

8. Experts in the field of personnel relations feel that it is generally a bad practice for subordinate employees to become aware of pending or contemplated changes in policy or organizational set-up via the "grapevine" CHIEFLY because 8.____

A. evidence that one or more responsible officials have proved untrustworthy will undermine confidence in the agency
B. the information disseminated by this method is seldom entirely accurate and generally spreads needless unrest among the subordinate staff
C. the subordinate staff may conclude that the administration feels the staff cannot be trusted with the true information
D. the subordinate staff may conclude that the administration lacks the courage to make an unpopular announcement through official channels

9. Assume that a supervisor praises his subordinates for satisfactory aspects of their work only when he is about to criticize them for unsatisfactory aspects of their work. Such a practice is UNDESIRABLE primarily because 9.____

A. his subordinates may expect to be praised for their work even if it is unsatisfactory
B. praising his subordinates for some aspects of their work while criticizing other aspects will weaken the effects of the criticisms
C. his subordinates would be more receptive to criticism if it were followed by praise
D. his subordinates may come to disregard praise and wait for criticism to be given

10. The one of the following which would be the BEST reason for an agency to eliminate a procedure for obtaining and recording certain information is that 10.____

A. it is no longer legally required to obtain the information
B. there is an advantage in obtaining the information
C. the information could be compiled on the basis of other information available
D. the information obtained is sometimes incorrect

11. In determining the type and number of records to be kept in an agency, it is important to recognize that records are of value PRIMARILY as 11.____

A. raw material to be used in statistical analysis
B. sources of information about the agency's activities
C. by-products of the activities carried on by the agency
D. data for evaluating the effectiveness of the agency

12. Assume that you are a supervisor. One of the workers under your supervision is careless about the routine aspects of his work. 12.____
Of the following, the action MOST likely to develop in this worker a better attitude toward job routines is to demonstrate that

A. it is just as easy to do his job the right way
B. organization of his job will leave more time for field work
C. the routine part of the job is essential to performing a good piece of work
D. job routines are a responsibility of the worker

13. A supervisor can MOST effectively secure necessary improvement in a worker's office work by 13.____

A. encouraging the worker to keep abreast of his work
B. relating the routine part of his job to the total job to be done
C. helping the worker to establish a good system for covering his office work and holding him to it
D. informing the worker that he will be required to organize his work more efficiently

14. A supervisor should offer criticism in such a manner that the criticism is helpful and not overwhelming. 14.____
Of the following, the LEAST valid inference that can be drawn on the basis of the above statement is that a supervisor should

A. demonstrate that the criticism is partial and not total
B. give criticism in such a way that it does not undermine the worker's self-confidence
C. keep his relationships with the worker objective
D. keep criticism directed towards general work performance

15. The one of the following areas in which a worker may LEAST reasonably expect direct assistance from the supervisor is in 15.____

A. building up rapport with all clients
B. gaining insight into the unmet needs of clients
C. developing an understanding of community resources
D. interpreting agency policies and procedures

16. You are informed that a worker under your supervision has submitted a letter complaining of unfair service rating. Of the following, the MOST valid assumption for you to make concerning this worker is that he should be 16.____

A. more adequately supervised in the future
B. called in for a supervisory conference
C. given a transfer to some other unit where he may be more happy
D. given no more consideration than any other inefficient worker

17. Assume that you are a supervisor. You find that a somewhat bewildered worker, newly appointed to the department, hesitates to ask questions for fear of showing his ignorance and jeopardizing his position. 17.____
Of the following, the BEST procedure for you to follow is to

A. try to discover the reason for his evident fear of authority
B. tell him that when he is in doubt about a procedure or a policy he should consult his fellow workers
C. develop with the worker a plan for more frequent supervisory conferences
D. explain why each staff member is eager to give him available information that will help him do a good job

18. In order to teach an employee to develop an objective approach, the BEST action for the supervisor to take is to help the worker to 18.____

A. develop a sincere interest in his job
B. understand the varied responsibilities that are an integral part of his job
C. differentiate clearly between himself as a friend and as an employee
D. find satisfaction in his work

19. Of the following, the MOST effective method of helping a newly appointed employee adjust to his new job is to 19.____

A. assure him that with experience his uncertain attitudes will be replaced by a professional approach
B. help him, by accepting him as he is, to have confidence in his ability to handle the job
C. help him to be on guard against the development of punitive attitudes
D. help him to recognize the mutability of the agency's policies and procedures

20. Suppose that, as a supervisor, you have scheduled an individual conference with an experienced employee under your supervision. 20.____
Of the following, the BEST plan of action for this conference is to

A. discuss the work that the employee is most interested in
B. plan with the employee to cover any problems that are difficult for him
C. advise the employee that the conference is his to do with as he sees fit
D. spot check the employee's work in advance and select those areas for discussion in which the employee has done poor work

21. Of the following, the CHIEF function of a supervisor should be to 21.____

A. assist in the planning of new policies and the evaluation of existing ones
B. promote congenial relationships among members of the staff
C. achieve optimum functioning of each unit and each worker
D. promote the smooth functioning of job routines

22. The competent supervisor must realize the importance of planning. 22.____
Of the following, the aspect of planning which is LEAST appropriately considered a responsibility of the supervisor is

A. long-range planning for the proper functioning of his unit
B. planning to take care of peak and slack periods
C. planning to cover agency policies in group conferences

D. long-range planning to develop community resources

23. The one of the following objectives which should be of LEAST concern to the supervisor in the performance of his duties is to 23.____

A. help the worker to make friends with all of his fellow employees
B. be impartial and fair to all members of the staff
C. stimulate the worker's growth on the job
D. meet the needs of the individual employee

24. The one of the following which is LEAST properly considered a direct responsibility of the supervisor is 24.____

A. liaison between the staff and the administrator
B. interpreting administrative orders and procedures to the employee
C. training new employees
D. maintaining staff morale at a high level

25. If an employee shows excessive submission which indicates a need for dependence on the supervisor in handling an assignment, it would be MOST advisable for the supervisor to 25.____

A. indicate firmly that the employee-supervisor relationship does not call for submission
B. define areas of responsibility of employee and of superior
C. recognize the employee's need to be sustained and supported and help him by making decisions for him
D. encourage the employee to do his best to overcome his handicap

---

KEY (CORRECT ANSWERS)

1. B
2. A
3. B
4. C
5. D

6. D
7. D
8. B
9. D
10. C

11. B
12. D
13. B
14. D
15. A

16. B
17. C
18. C
19. B
20. B

21. C
22. D
23. A
24. A
25. B

TEST 2

DIRECTIONS: Each question or incomplete statement is followed by several suggested answers or completions. Select the one that BEST answers the question or completes the statement. *PRINT THE LETTER OF THE CORRECT ANSWER IN THE SPACE AT THE RIGHT.*

1. Assume that, as a supervisor, you are conducting a group conference. Of the following, the BEST procedure for you to follow in order to stimulate group discussion is to 1.____

   A. permit the active participation of all members
   B. direct the discussion to an acceptable conclusion
   C. resolve conflicts of opinion among members of the group
   D. present a question for discussion on which the group members have some knowledge or experience

2. Suppose that, as a new supervisor, you wish to inform the staff under your supervision of your methods of operation. Of the following, the BEST procedure for you to follow is to 2.____

   A. advise the staff that they will learn gradually from experience
   B. inform each employee in an individual conference
   C. call a group conference for this purpose
   D. distribute a written memorandum among all members of the staff

3. The MOST constructive and effective method of correcting an employee who has made a mistake is, in general, to 3.____

   A. explain that his evaluation is related to his errors
   B. point out immediately where he erred and tell him how it should have been done
   C. show him how to readjust his methods so as to avoid similar errors in the future
   D. try to discover by an indirect method why the error was made

4. The MOST effective method for the supervisor to follow in order to obtain the cooperation of an employee under his supervision is, wherever possible, to 4.____

   A. maintain a careful record of performance in order to keep the employee on his toes
   B. give the employee recognition in order to promote greater effort and give him more satisfaction in his work
   C. try to gain the employee's cooperation for the good of the service
   D. advise the employee that his advancement on the job depends on his cooperation

5. Of the following, the MOST appropriate initial course for an employee to take when he is unable to clarify a policy with his supervisor is to 5.____

   A. bring up the problem at the next group conference
   B. discuss the policy immediately with his fellow employees
   C. accept the supervisor's interpretation as final
   D. determine what responsibility he has for putting the policy into effect

6. Good administration allows for different treatment of different workers. Of the following, the CHIEF implication of this quotation is that 6.____

A. it would be unfair for the supervisor not to treat all staff members alike
B. fear of favoritism tends to undermine staff morale
C. best results are obtained by individualization within the limits of fair treatment
D. difficult problems call for a different kind of approach

7. The MOST effective and appropriate method of building efficiency and morale in a group of employees is, in general, 7.____

A. by stressing the economic motive
B. through use of the authority inherent in the position
C. by a friendly approach to all
D. by a discipline that is fair but strict

8. Of the following, the LEAST valid basis for the assignment of work to an employee is the 8.____

A. kind of service to be rendered
B. experience and training of the employee
C. health and capacity of the employee
D. racial composition of the community where the office is located

9. The CHIEF justification for staff education, consisting of in-service training, lies in its contribution to 9.____

A. improvement in the quality of work performed
B. recruitment of a better type of employee
C. employee morale accruing from a feeling of growth on the job
D. the satisfaction that the employee gets on his job

10. Suppose that you are a supervisor. An employee no longer with your department requests you, as his former supervisor, to write a letter recommending him for a position with a private organization. 10.____
Of the following, the BEST procedure for you to follow is to include in the letter only information that

A. will help the applicant get the job
B. is clear, factual, and substantiated
C. is known to you personally
D. can readily be corroborated by personal interview

11. Of the following, the MOST important item on which to base the efficiency evaluation of an employee under your supervision is 11.____

A. the nature of the relationship that he has built up with his fellow employees
B. how he gets along with his supervisors
C. his personal habits and skills
D. the effectiveness of his control over his work

12. According to generally accepted personnel practice, the MOST effective method of building morale in a new employee is to 12.____

A. exercise caution in praising the employee, lest he become overconfident
B. give sincere and frank commendation whenever possible, in order to stimulate interest and effort

C. praise the employee highly even for mediocre performance so that he will be stimulated to do better
D. warn the employee frequently that he cannot hope to succeed unless he puts forth his best effort

13. Errors made by newly appointed employees often follow a predictable pattern. The one of the following errors likely to have LEAST serious consequences is the tendency of a new employee to 13.___

A. discuss problems that are outside his province with the client
B. persuade the client to accept the worker's solution of a problem
C. be too strict in carrying out departmental policy and procedure
D. depend upon the use of authority due to his inexperience and lack of skill in working with people

14. The MOST effective way for a supervisor to break down a worker's defensive stand against supervisory guidance is to 14.___

A. come to an understanding with him on the mutual responsibilities involved in the job of the employee and supervisor
B. tell him he must feel free to express his opinions and to discuss basic problems
C. show him how to develop toward greater objectivity, sensitivity, and understanding
D. advise him that it is necessary to carry out agency policy and procedures in order to do a good job

15. Of the following, the LEAST essential function of the supervisor who is conducting a group conference should be to 15.___

A. keep attention focused on the purpose of the conference
B. encourage discussion of controversial points
C. make certain that all possible viewpoints are discussed
D. be thoroughly prepared in advance

16. When conducting a group conference, the supervisor should be LEAST concerned with 16.___

A. providing an opportunity for the free interchange of ideas
B. imparting knowledge and understanding of case work
C. leading the discussion toward a planned goal
D. pointing out where individual workers have erred in work practice

17. If the participants in a group conference are unable to agree on the proper application of a concept to the work of a department, the MOST suitable temporary procedure for the supervisor to follow is to 17.___

A. suggest that each member think the subject through before the next meeting
B. tell the group to examine their differences for possible conflicts with present policies
C. suggest that practices can be changed because of new conditions
D. state the acceptable practice in the agency and whether deviations from such practice can be permitted

18. If an employee is to participate constructively in any group discussion, it is MOST important that he have 18.____

   A. advance notice of the agenda for the meeting
   B. long experience in the department
   C. knowledge and experience in the particular work
   D. the ability to assume a leadership role

19. Of the following, the MOST important principle for the supervisor to follow when conducting a group discussion is that he should 19.____

   A. move the discussion toward acceptance by the group of a particular point of view
   B. express his ideas clearly and succinctly
   C. lead the group to accept the authority inherent in his position
   D. contribute to the discussion from his knowledge and experience

20. The one of the following which is considered LEAST important as a purpose of the group conference is to 20.____

   A. provide for a free exchange of ideas among the members of the group
   B. evaluate work methods and procedures in order to protect the members from individual criticism
   C. provide an opportunity to interpret procedures and work practices
   D. pool the experience of the group members for the benefit of all

21. In order for the evaluation conference to stimulate MOST effectively the employee's professional growth on the job, it should 21.____

   A. start him thinking, about his present status with the department
   B. show him the necessity for taking stock of his total performance
   C. give him a sense of direction in relation to his future development
   D. give him a better perspective on the work in his department

22. The development of good public relations in the area for which the supervisor is responsible should be considered by the supervisor as 22.____

   A. not his responsibility as he is primarily responsible for his employees' services
   B. dependent upon him as he is in the best position to interpret the department to the community
   C. not important to the adequate functioning of the department
   D. a part of his method of carrying out his job responsibility, as what his employees do affect the community

23. Of the following, the MOST valuable and desirable trait in a supervisor is a(n) 23.____

   A. ability to get the best work out of his men
   B. ability to inspire his men with the desire to "get ahead in the world"
   C. persuasive manner of speech
   D. tall and commanding appearance

24. The supervisor who is MOST suitable for the general practical needs of a department is the one who gets 24.___

    A. a great deal of satisfactory work done although usually handicapped by constant bickering among fellow employees
    B. a great deal of satisfactory work done because of his ability to do a large amount of it himself
    C. less work done than the other supervisors but has unusually high quality work production standards
    D. more than an average amount of satisfactory work done because of the cooperative way in which the employees work for him

25. A supervisor has been transferred to a new section. 25.___
The BEST way for him to get cooperation from his employees would be to

    A. ask the (general manager)(chief) to give him strong support
    B. explain his policy firmly so that the employees cannot blame him for any mistakes made
    C. note the troublemakers and have them transferred out
    D. show his men that he not only is interested in getting work done but also has their welfare in mind

KEY (CORRECT ANSWERS)

1.	D	11.	D
2.	C	12.	B
3.	C	13.	C
4.	B	14.	A
5.	D	15.	B
6.	C	16.	D
7.	D	17.	D
8.	D	18.	A
9.	A	19.	D
10.	B	20.	B

21.	C
22.	D
23.	A
24.	D
25.	D

TEST 3

DIRECTIONS: Each question or incomplete statement is followed by several suggested answers or completions. Select the one that BEST answers the question or completes the statement. *PRINT THE LETTER OF THE CORRECT ANSWER IN THE SPACE AT THE RIGHT.*

1. Jones and Smith, who work together, do slightly more than an average amount of work for two men together. But you find that Jones does most of the work while Smith does less than he should. 1.____
   To correct this situation, the BEST thing for you as supervisor to do would be to

   A. assign work to Smith for which he must be personally responsible
   B. make a complaint to the bureau chief about Smith but praise Jones
   C. point out to Jones that he does most of the work and that he should urge Smith to do more
   D. require Smith to do more whenever the work of both men together falls below the expected average

2. You have given a new employee detailed instructions on how he should do a job. When you return a little later, you find that the employee was afraid to start the job because he did not completely understand your instructions. 2.____
   In this situation, it would be BEST for you to

   A. assign the man to a job where less intelligence is needed
   B. explain again, illustrating if possible how the job is to be done
   C. explain again and recommend him for dropping at the end of probation if he does not understand
   D. make the man explain why he did not at least start the job

3. An employee does very good work but has trouble getting to work on time. 3.____
   To get him to come on time, the supervisor should

   A. bring him up on charges to stop the lateness once and for all
   B. have him report to the general manager every time he is late
   C. talk over the problem with him to find its cause and possible solution
   D. threaten to transfer him if he cannot get to work early

4. As supervisor, you observe that an employee keeps making mistakes. 4.____
   Of the following, the BEST thing for you to do would be to

   A. make no mention of these mistakes as they gradually disappear with experience
   B. point the mistakes out to the employee in front of the other employees so all may learn from them
   C. talk to the employee privately about these mistakes and show her how to avoid them
   D. try to transfer this employee out in exchange for an employee who can do the work

5. Proper action by the supervisor could MOST probably prevent work delays in his section caused by 5.____

   A. a large number of employees quitting their jobs in the department
   B. the daily assignments of the employees not being properly planned

C. the inexperience of new employees transferred into his section
D. unexpected delays in processing

6. If, after careful thought, you have definitely decided that one of your employees should be disciplined, it is MOST important for you to realize that 6.___

A. discipline is the best tool for leading workers
B. discipline should be severe in order to get the best results
C. the discipline should be delayed so that its full force can be felt
D. the employee should know why she is being disciplined

7. A knowledge of the experience and abilities of the men working under him is MOST useful to a supervisor in 7.___

A. deciding what type of discipline to exercise when necessary
B. finding the cause of minor errors in the assignments
C. making proper work assignments
D. making vacation schedules

8. A supervisor will be able to train his employees better if he is familiar with basic principles of learning. 8.___
Which one of the following statements about the learning process is MOST correct?

A. An employee who learns one job quickly will learn any other job quickly.
B. Emphasizing correct things done by the employee usually gives him an incentive to improve.
C. Great importance placed on an employee's mistakes is the best way to help him to get rid of them.
D. It is very hard to teach new methods to middle-aged or older employees.

9. Several experienced employees have resigned. You have decided to arrange for permanent transfers of other experienced employees in your section to fill their jobs, leaving only jobs that new inexperienced employees can fill easily. 9.___
For you, the supervisor, to talk this over with the employees who will be affected by the move would be

A. *bad;* it would show weakness and wavering by you
B. *bad;* transfers should be made on the basis of efficiency
C. *good;* it will help you get better cooperation from the employees involved
D. *good;* transfers should be made on the basis of seniority

10. An employee under your supervision does much less work than he is capable of. 10.___
What should be your FIRST step in an effort to improve his performance?

A. Discovering why he is not working up to his full capacity
B. Going over his mistakes and shortcomings with him to reduce them
C. Pointing out to him that the quality of his work is below standard
D. Showing him that the other men produce much more than he does

11. The FIRST thing a supervisor does when he assigns an employee to a new job is to find out what the employee already knows about the job. 11.___
This practice is

A. *good;* mainly because the employees may know more than the supervisor about the job
B. *good;* mainly because this information will help the supervisor in instructing the employee
C. *poor;* mainly because since it is a new job, the employee cannot be expected to know anything
D. *poor;* mainly because the supervisor should first find out how the employee will feel toward the job

12. Your superior has assigned to you a task which, in your opinion, should not be performed at this stage of the operation. 12.____
In this situation, it would be BEST for you to

A. carry out the assignment since your superior is responsible
B. refuse to carry out the assignment
C. talk it over with the employees under you to see if they think as you do
D. talk the matter over with your superior right away

13. It is important for a supervisor to take prompt action upon requests from subordinates MAINLY because 13.____

A. delays in making decisions mean that they must then be made on the basis of facts which can no longer be up-to-date
B. favorable action on such requests is more likely to result when a decision is made quickly
C. it is an indication that the supervisor has his work well-organized
D. promptness in such matters helps maintain good employee morale

14. As a supervisor, you realize that your superior, when under pressure, has a habit of giving you oral orders which are not always clear and also lack sufficient detail. The BEST procedure for you to follow in such situations would be to 14.____

A. obtain clarification by requesting needed details at the time you receive such orders
B. consider past orders of a similar nature to determine the probable intent of your superior
C. frequently consult your superior during the course of the job in order to secure the required details to complete the job
D. request your superior to put all his orders to you in writing

15. Some supervisors have their subordinates meet with them in group discussion of troublesome problems. 15.____
The MAIN advantage of such group discussions as a supervisory tool is that they can be directed toward the

A. appraisal of the personalities involved
B. development of new policies and regulations
C. circulation of new material and information
D. pooling of experience in the solution of common problems

16. The PRINCIPAL disadvantage of using form letters to reply to written complaints made by the public is that such form letters 16.____

A. tend to make any investigation of the original complaint rather superficial
B. are limited by their design to handle only a few possible situations that could give rise to complaints
C. lack the desirable element of the personal touch for the recipient
D. tend to lose their effectiveness by quickly becoming obsolete

17. With respect to standard employee grievance procedure, it would be MOST correct to state that 17.____

A. the Commissioner of Labor is the highest ranking official, excepting the judge, who can be involved in a particular grievance
B. the person with the grievance has the right to be represented by virtually anyone he chooses
C. the one having the grievance (the grievant) can be represented by the majority organization only if he is a member thereof
D. time limits are not set concerning adjudication in order to insure the fullest consideration of the particular grievance

18. In order for a supervisor to employ the system of democratic leadership in his supervision, it would generally be BEST for him to 18.____

A. allow his subordinates to assist in deciding on methods of work performance and job assignments but only in those areas where decisions have not been made on higher administrative levels
B. allow his subordinates to decide how to do the required work, interposing his authority when work is not completed on schedule or is improperly completed
C. attempt to make assignments of work to individuals only of the type which they enjoy doing
D. maintain control over the job assignments and work production but allow the subordinates to select methods of work and internal conditions of work at democratically conducted staff conferences

19. In an office in which supervision has been considered quite effective, it has become necessary to press for above-normal production for a limited period to achieve a required goal. 19.____
The one of the following which is a LEAST likely result of this pressure is that

A. there will be more "gripings" by employees
B. some workers will do both more and better work than has been normal for them
C. there will be an enhanced feeling of group unity
D. there will be increased absenteeism

20. It is the practice of some supervisors, when they believe that it would be desirable for a subordinate to take a particular action in a case, to inform the subordinate of this in the form of a suggestion rather than in the form of a direct order. In general, this method of getting a subordinate to take the desired action is 20.____

A. *inadvisable;* it may create in the mind of the subordinate the impression that the supervisor is uncertain about the efficacy of his plan and is trying to avoid whatever responsibility he may have in resolving the case
B. *advisable;* it provides the subordinate with the maximum opportunity to use his own judgment in handling the case

C. *inadvisable;* it provides the subordinate with no clear-cut direction and, therefore, is likely to leave him with a feeling of uncertainty and frustration
D. *advisable;* it presents the supervisor's view in a manner which will be most likely to evoke the subordinate's cooperation

21. At a group training conference conducted by a supervisor, one of the employees asks a question which is only partially related to the subject under discussion. He believes that the question was asked to embarrass him since he recently reprimanded the employees for inattention to his work. Under these circumstances, it would generally be BEST for the assistant supervisor to 21.____

A. pointedly ignore the question and the questioner and go on to other matters
B. request the questioner to remain after the group session, at which time the question and the questioner's attitude will be considered
C. state that he does not know the answer and ask for a volunteer to give a brief answer, brief because the question is only partially relevant
D. tell the questioner that the question is not pertinent, show wherein it is not pertinent, and state that the time of the group should not be wasted on it

22. The one of the following circumstances when it would generally be MOST proper for a supervisor to do a job himself rather than to train a subordinate to do the job is when it is 22.____

A. a job which the supervisor enjoys doing and does well
B. not a very time-consuming job but an important one
C. difficult to train another to do the job yet is not difficult for the supervisor to do
D. unlikely that this or any similar job will have to be done again at any future time

23. Effective training of subordinates requires that the supervisor understand certain facts about learning and forgetting processes. 23.____
Among these is the fact that people generally

A. both learn and forget at a relatively constant rate and this rate is dependent upon their general intellectual capacity
B. forget what they learned at a much greater rate during the first day than during subsequent periods
C. learn at a relatively constant rate except for periods of assimilation when the quantity of retained learning decreases while information is becoming firmly fixed in the mind
D. learn very slowly at first when introduced to a new topic, after which there is a great increase in the rate of learning

24. It has been suggested that a subordinate who likes his supervisor will tend to do better work than one who does not. According to the MOST widely-held current theories of supervision, this suggestion is a 24.____

A. *bad one;* since personal relationships tend to interfere with proper professional relationships
B. *bad one;* since the strongest motivating factors are fear and uncertainty
C. *good one;* since liking one's supervisor is a motivating factor for good work performance
D. *good one;* since liking one's supervisor is the most important factor in employee performance

25. A supervisor is supervising an employee who is very soon to complete his six months' probationary period. The supervisor finds him to be slow, to make many errors, to do work poorly, to be antagonistic toward the supervisor, and to be disliked by most of his co-workers. The supervisor is aware that he is the sole support of his wife and two children. He has never been late or absent during his service with the department. If he is terminated, there will be a considerable delay before a replacement for him arrives. It would generally be BEST for the supervisor to recommend that this employee be 25.____

A. transferred to work with another supervisor and other staff members with whom he may get along better
B. retained but be very closely supervised until his work shows marked improvement
C. retained since his services are needed with the expectation that he be terminated at some later date when a replacement is readily available
D. terminated

KEY (CORRECT ANSWERS)

1. A
2. B
3. C
4. C
5. B
6. D
7. C
8. B
9. C
10. A
11. B
12. D
13. D
14. A
15. D
16. C
17. B
18. A
19. D
20. D
21. C
22. D
23. B
24. C
25. D

EXAMINATION SECTION

TEST 1

DIRECTIONS: Each question or incomplete statement is followed by several suggested answers or completions. Select the one that BEST answers the question or completes the statement. *PRINT THE LETTER OF THE CORRECT ANSWER IN THE SPACE AT THE RIGHT.*

1. From time to time, your subordinates are assigned to other units to do reception work and other duties. You receive a note from Mr. Jones, the head of one of these other units, stating that the work of Miss Smith, one of your subordinates, was unsatisfactory when she worked for him, and asking you not to assign her to him again. Although Miss Smith has worked in your unit for a long time, this is the first time that anyone has complained about her work. 1.____
   The one of the following actions that you should take FIRST in this situation is to ask
   A. the heads of the other units for whom Miss Smith has worked whether or not her work has been satisfactory
   B. Mr. Jones in what way Miss Smith's work has been unsatisfactory
   C. Miss Smith to explain in what way her work for Mr. Jones was unsatisfactory
   D. Mr. Jones which of your subordinates he would prefer to have assigned to him

2. Suppose that you are the supervisor of a small unit in a city agency. You have given one of your subordinates, Mr. Smith, an assignment which must be completed by the end of the day. Because he is unfamiliar with the assignment, Mr. Smith will be unable to complete it on time. Your other subordinates are too busy to help Mr. Smith, but you have the time to help him complete the assignment. 2.____
   For you to help Mr. Smith complete the assignment would be
   A. *desirable*; because a supervisor is expected to be familiar with his subordinates' work
   B. *undesirable*; because Mr. Smith will come to depend on you to help him do his work
   C. *desirable*; because Mr. Smith is likely to appreciate your help and give you his cooperation when you need it
   D. *undesirable*; because a supervisor should not perform the same type of work as his subordinates do

3. For a supervisor to listen to the personal problems which his subordinates bring to him is GENERALLY 3.____
   A. *desirable*; it is likely that the supervisor has broader experience in solving personal problems than do his subordinates
   B. *undesirable*; the supervisor may be unable to solve such problems

C. *desirable*; the supervisor can better understand his subordinates' behavior on the job
D. *undesirable*; permitting a subordinate to talk about his personal problems may only make them seem worse

4. A generally accepted concept of management is that the authority given to a person should be commensurate with his 4.____
A. responsibility
B. ability
C. seniority
D. dependability

5. It has been said that the best supervisor is the one who gives the fewest orders. The one of the following supervisor practices that would be MOT likely to increase the number of orders that a supervisor must give to get out the work is to 5.____
A. set general goals for his subordinates and give them the authority for reaching the goals
B. train subordinates to make decisions for themselves
C. establish routines for his subordinates' jobs
D. introduce frequent changes in the work methods his subordinates are using

6. The one of the following supervisory practices that would be MOST likely to give subordinates a feeling of satisfaction in their work is to 6.____
A. establish work goals that take a long time to achieve
B. show the subordinates how their work goals are related to the goals of the agency
C. set work goals higher than the subordinates can achieve
D. refrain from telling the subordinates that they are failing to meet their work goals

7. You are about to design a system for measuring the quantity of work produced by your subordinates. 7.____
The one of the following which is the FIRST step that you should take in designing this system is to
A. establish the units of work measurement to be used in the system
B. determine the actual advantages and disadvantages of the system
C. determine the abilities of each of your subordinates
D. ascertain the types of work done in the unit

8. One of your subordinates tells you that he is dissatisfied with his work assignment and that he wishes to discuss the matter with you. The employee is obviously very angry and upset. 8.____
Of the following, the course of action that you should take FIRST in this situation is to
A. postpone discussion of the employee's complaint, explaining to him that the matter can be settled more satisfactorily if it is discussed calmly
B. have the employee describe his complaint, correcting him whenever he makes what seems to be an erroneous charge against you

C. permit the employee to present his complaint in full, withholding your comments until he has finished describing his complaint
D. promise the employee that you will review all the work assignments in the unit to determine whether or not any changes should be made

9. Assume that you are the supervisor of a unit in a city agency. One of your subordinates has violated an important rule of the agency. For such a violation, you are required to impose discipline in the form of a reprimand given in private. 9.____
Of the following, the MOST important reason for disciplining the employee for violating the rule is to
A. obtain his compliance with the rule
B. punish him for his action in an impartial manner
C. establish your authority to administer discipline
D. impress upon all the employees in the unit the need for observing the rule

10. You are the newly appointed supervisor of a small unit in a city agency. One of your subordinates, Mr. Smith, a competent employee, has resented your appointment as his supervisor and has not been as cooperative toward you as you have wanted him to be. One day, Mr. Smith fails to observe an important rule of the agency. You are required to reprimand any employee who fails to observe the rule. 10.____
The one of the following courses of action you should take in this situation is to
A. attempt to overcome Mr. Smith's resentment by explaining to him that although you should reprimand him, you will not do so
B. reprimand Mr. Smith after pointing out to him that he failed to observe the rule
C. tell Mr. Smith that if he becomes more cooperative, you will overlook his failure to observe the rule
D. tell Mr. Smith that although you did not originate the rule, nevertheless you are required to reprimand him

11. Suppose that a clerk who has injured himself on the job because of his carelessness informs his supervisor of the accident. The supervisor has been newly appointed to his job and is anxious to keep accidents at a minimum. The action taken by the supervisor is to criticize the subordinate for his carelessness and to tell him that he is holding him responsible for the accident. 11.____
Of the following, it would be MOST reasonable to conclude that, as a result of the supervisor's action, his subordinates may
A. tend to withhold information from him about future accidents
B. be critical of him, in turn, if he himself is injured on the job
C. expect him to supervise them more closely in the future
D. attempt to correct hazardous job conditions without his knowledge

12. The one of the following which is GENERALLY the basic reason for using standard procedures in an agency is to 12.____
A. provide sequences of steps for handling recurring activities
B. facilitate periodic review of standard practices

C. train new employees in the agency's policies and objectives
D. serve as a basis for formulating agency policies

13. Assume that the operations of a certain unit in an agency enable the supervisor to allow each of his subordinates wide discretion in selecting the kind and amount of work he chooses to do. However, in evaluating the work of his subordinates, the supervisor places more emphasis on some area of work than on others. Factors such as number of applications processed and number of letters written are given great weight in evaluation, while factors such as number of papers filed and number of forms checked are given little weight. Hence, a subordinate who processes a large number of applications would receive a high evaluation even if he checked very few forms. 13.____
The supervisor's method of evaluation would MOST likely result in a(n)
    A. increase in the amount of time spent on processing each application
    B. backlog of papers waiting to be filed
    C. improvement in the quality of letters written
    D. decline in output in all areas of work

14. Some management authorities propose that work assignments be made by assigning a varied set of tasks to a group of employees and then allowing the group to decide for itself how to organize the work to be done. This method of assigning work is called *job enlargement*. 14.____
The one of the following which is considered to be the CHIEF advantage of job enlargement is that it
    A. encourages employees to specialize in the work they are assigned to do
    B. reduces the amount of control that employees have over their work
    C. increases the employees' job satisfaction
    D. reduces the number of skills that each employee is required to learn

15. In conducting a meeting to pass along information to his subordinates, a supervisor may talk to his subordinates without giving them the opportunity to interrupt him. This method is called one-way communication. On the other hand, the supervisor may talk to his subordinates and give them the opportunity to ask questions or make comments while he is speaking. This method is called two-way communication. 15.____
It would be MORE desirable for the supervisor to use two-way communication rather than one-way communication at a meeting when his primary purpose is to
    A. avoid, during the meeting, open criticism of any mistakes he may make
    B. conduct the meeting in an orderly fashion
    C. pass along information quickly
    D. transmit information which must be clearly understood

16. Assume that you are the leader of a training conference on supervisory techniques and problems. One of the participants in the conference proposes what you consider to be an unsatisfactory technique for handling the problem under discussion. 16.____

The one of the following courses of action which you should take in this situation is to

A. explain to the participants why the proposed technique is unsatisfactory
B. stimulate the other participants to discuss the appropriateness of the proposed technique
C. proceed immediately to another problem without discussing the proposed technique
D. end further discussion of the problem but explain to the participant in private, after the conference is over, why he proposed technique is unsatisfactory

17. In measuring the work of his subordinates, the supervisor of a unit performing routine filing began by observing his subordinates at work. If a subordinate seemed to be busy, then the supervisor concluded that the subordinate was producing a great deal of work. On the other hand, the supervisor concluded that a subordinate was not producing much work if he did not seem to be busy. The supervisor's work measurement method was faulted CHIEFLY because 17.____

A. it did not use a standard against which a subordinate's work could be measured
B. the type of work performed by his subordinates did not lend itself to accurate measurement
C. his subordinates may not have worked at their normal rates if they were aware that their work was being observed
D. the supervisor may not have observed a subordinate's work for a long enough period of time

18. Assume that a system of statistical reports designed to provide information about employee work performance is put into effect in a unit of a city agency. There is some evidence that the employees of this unit are working below their capacities. The information obtained from the system is to be used by management to improve employee work and performance and to evaluate such performance. The employees whose work is to be recorded by the reports resent them. Nevertheless, the employees' work performance improves substantially after the reporting system is put into effect, and before management has put the information to use.
The one of the following which is the MOST accurate conclusion to be drawn from this situation is that 18.____

A. a statistical reporting system may fail to provide the information it is designed to provide
B. low employee morale may have been the cause of the employees' former level of work performance
C. a statistical reporting system designed only to provide information about problems may also help to solve the problems
D. willing employee cooperation is essential to the success of a system of statistical reports

19. In setting the work standard for a certain task, a unit supervisor took the total output of all the employees in the unit and divided it by the number of employees. He thus established the average output as the work standard for the task. 19.____
The method that the supervisor used to establish the work standard is GENERALLY considered to be
   A. *proper,* since the method takes into account the output of the outstanding, as well as of the less productive, employees
   B. *improper*, since the average output may not be what could reasonably be expected of a competent, satisfactory employee
   C. *proper*, since the standard is based on the actual output of the employees who are to be evaluated
   D. *improper*, since all the employees in the unit may be successful in meeting the work standard

20. There are disadvantages as well as advantages in using statistical controls to measure specific aspects of subordinates' jobs. 20.____
The one of the following which can LEAST be considered to be an advantage of statistical controls to a supervisor is that such controls may
   A. reduce the need for close, detailed supervision
   B. give the supervisor information that he needs for making decisions
   C. stimulate subordinates whose work is measured by statistical controls to improve their performance
   D. encourage subordinates to emphasize aspects being measured rather than their jobs as a whole

21. Mr. Stone, who has been recently placed in charge of a clerical unit staffed with ten employees, plans to institute several radical changes in the procedures of his unit. 21.____
Of the following actions he may take before adopting any of the revisions, the MOST desirable one is for Mr. Stone to
   A. distribute to each staff member a memorandum describing the revised procedures and requesting the staff's cooperation in giving the revised procedures a fair trial
   B. issue to each staff member a memorandum describing the proposed changes and inviting him to submit his written criticism of these proposed changes
   C. issue to each staff member a memorandum describing the proposed changes and notifying him of the time and date of a staff conference to be held on the merits
   D. of the proposed changes discuss the proposed changes with each staff member independently and obtain his opinion of the proposed changes

22. An assignment completed by Frank King is returned to him by his unit supervisor for certain changes. Frank King objects to making these changes. 22.____
Of the following, the MOST appropriate action for the unit supervisor to take FIRST is to
   A. permit Frank King to present his arguments against making these changes

B. inform Frank King that he is free to take the matter up with a higher authority
C. reprimand Frank King for objecting and assign another employee to make these changes
D. state briefly that his decision is final and indicate by his manner that further discussion would be useless

23. Of the following, it is LEAST essential for a supervisor, in assigning work to a subordinate, to issue written instructions when the 23.____
A. supervisor will be on hand to check the work
B. instructions are to be passed on to other employees
C. assignment involves many details
D. subordinate is to be held strictly accountable for the work performed

24. Assume that you have been placed in charge of a unit where the quality of the work performed is poor. You plan to discuss the matter of improving the quality of the wok at a staff meeting of the unit. 24.____
Of the following courses of action which you might take at this meeting, the BEST one is to
A. describe a few cases of exceptionally poor work performance; then have the employees performing this work explain why their work was done poorly
B. inform the staff that you will be criticized by your own superior if the quality of the unit's work does not improve; then discuss, in general terms, the problem of improving the quality of the work
C. discuss the problem of improving the quality of the unit's work; then call upon each employee by name for his suggestions for improving the work he performs
D. present the problem to the staff; then indicate and discuss specific methods for improving the quality of the work

25. Suppose that certain office responsibilities require you to be frequently absent from the unit you supervise. You have, therefore, decided to designate one of your staff members to act as unit head in your absence. 25.____
Of the following factors, the one which is MOST important in selecting the employee best fitted for this assignment is his
A. manner and personal appearance
B. estimated ability to perform work of a supervisory nature
C. ability to perform his present duties
D. relative seniority in the service

KEY (CORRECT ANSWERS)

1. B
2. C
3. C
4. A
5. D

6. B
7. D
8. C
9. A
10. B

11. A
12. A
13. B
14. C
15. D

16. B
17. A
18. C
19. B
20. D

21. C
22. A
23. A
24. D
25. B

TEST 2

DIRECTIONS: Each question or incomplete statement is followed by several suggested answers or completions. Select the one that BEST answers the question or completes the statement. *PRINT THE LETTER OF THE CORRECT ANSWER IN THE SPACE AT THE RIGHT.*

1. Assume that your supervisor has placed you in complete charge of an important project and that several clerks have been assigned to assist you. You have been given authority to establish any new procedures or revise existing procedures in order to complete the project as soon as possible. Just before you begin work on the project, one of the clerks suggests a change in the procedure which you realize at once would result in completion of the project in about half the time you expected to spend on it. 1.____
Of the following, the MOST effective course of action for you to take is to
   A. adopt the suggestion immediately to expedite the completion of the project
   B. discuss the suggestion with your superior to obtain his consent to the change
   C. point out to the clerk that an adequate procedure has already been established, but that his suggestion may be used in future projects of this type
   D. encourage the other clerks to make further suggestions

2. A supervisor of a unit may safely delegate certain of his functions to his subordinates. 2.____
Of the following, the function which can MOST safely be delegated is the
   A. settlement of employee grievances
   B. planning and scheduling of the production of the unit
   C. improvement of production methods of the unit
   D. maintenance of records of the work output of the unit

3. Some organizations now question the effectiveness of extreme job specialization. It is felt that in some instances it may be more advantageous to enlarge the scope of individual jobs, thus providing the employee with a greater variety of tasks. 3.____
Of the following, the one which is LEAST likely to be a result of enlarging the scope of jobs is a(n)
   A. increase in the employee's job responsibilities
   B. decrease in the number of job titles in the organization
   C. increase in the number of tasks performed by an employee
   D. decrease in employee flexibility

4. A manual that is essentially designed to present detailed procedures and policies is not necessarily a good training medium, nor is a manual designed for high-level administrators likely to be satisfactory for use at lower levels. 4.____
The MOST valid implication of this quotation is that
   A. a manual, to be effective, should be flexible enough to apply to any working level in an organization

B. the uses to which a manual will be put and the people who will use it should be carefully determined before it is prepared
C. the more detailed procedures a manual contains, the more effective it will be for the use of administrators
D. the degree of difficulty encountered in the preparation of a manual varies with the purpose for which it is designed and the people for whom it is written

5. In assigning a complicated task to a group of subordinates, Mr. Jones, a unit supervisor, neither indicates the specific steps to be followed in performing the assignment nor designates the subordinate to be responsible for seeing that the task is done on time. 5.____
This supervisor's method of assigning the task is MOST likely to result in
A. the loss of skills previously acquired by his subordinates
B. assumption of authority by the most capable subordinates
C. friction and misunderstanding among subordinates with consequent delays in work
D. greater individual effort and self-reliance on the part of his subordinates

6. Assume that the head of your agency has appointed you to a committee that has been assigned the task of reviewing the clerical procedures used in a large bureau of the agency and of recommending appropriate changes in the procedures where necessary. 6.____
Of the following, the FIRST step that should be taken by the committee in carrying out its assignment is to
A. survey the most efficient procedures used in comparable agencies
B. study the organization of the bureau and the work it is required to do
C. evaluate the possible effects of proposed revisions in the procedures
D. determine the effectiveness of existing procedures

7. A recently developed practice in administration favors reducing the number of levels of authority in an organization, increasing the number of subordinates reporting to a superior, and also increasing the authority delegated to the subordinates. 7.____
This practice would MOST likely result in a(n)
A. increase in the span of control exercised by superiors
B. increase in detailed information that flows to a superior from each subordinate
C. decrease in the responsibility exercised by the subordinates
D. decrease in the number of functions performed by the subordinates

8. As an organization grows larger, the amount of personal contact between the top administrative officials and the rank and file employees diminishes. Consequently, management comes to rely more heavily upon written reports and records for securing information and exercising control. 8.____
The MOST valid implication of this quotation is that, as an organization grows larger,
A. evaluation of the work of rank and file employees becomes more objective because of greater reliance upon written reports and records

B. relations between first-line supervisors and their subordinates grow more impersonal
C. top administrative officials depend upon less direct methods for controlling the work of their subordinates
D. it becomes more difficult for top administrative officials to maintain high morale among rank and file employees

9. A supervisor whose unit has a good production record is usually found to be more occupied with the functions associated with leadership than with the performance of the same functions as his subordinates. 9.____
The MOST valid implication of this quotation is that
A. a supervisor whose unit has a good production record usually is not as competent in performing routine tasks as are his subordinates
B. ability to lead and competence in performing the day-to-day tasks of his subordinates are the requirements of a successful supervisor
C. a supervisor who spends more time on planning and organizing the work of his unit than on performing the routine tasks of his subordinates will find that a his unit's production record will be good
D. a supervisor whose unit has a good production record usually places less emphasis on performing the day-to-day tasks of his subordinates than on planning the work of his unit

10. To delegate work is one of the main functions of the supervisor. In delegating work, the supervisor should remember that even though an assignment is delegated to a subordinate, the supervisor ultimately is responsible for seeing that the work is done. 10.____
The MOST valid implication of this quotation for a supervisor is that he should
A. delegate as few difficult tasks as possible so as to minimize the consequences of inadequate performance by his subordinates
B. delegate to his subordinates those tasks which he considers difficult or time-consuming
C. check the progress of delegated assignments periodically to make certain that the work is being done properly
D. assign work to a subordinate without holding him directly accountable for carrying it out

11. A supervisor should select and develop an understudy to take charge of the unit in the supervisor's absence and to assist the supervisor whenever necessary. 11.____
Of the following, the technique that would be LEAST effective in developing an understudy is for the supervisor to
A. permit him to exercise complete supervision over certain parts of the work
B. assign him to work in which there is little likelihood of his making mistakes, so as to increase his self-confidence
C. accustom him to making reports on the progress of work he is supervising
D. give him responsibility gradually so that he will have time to absorb each new responsibility

12. A procedure manual of an agency is potentially more usable than are files of individual messages or bulletins, but usability and usefulness are not routine by-products of the manual form. 12.____
The MOST valid implication of this is that
    A. the purpose of a manual should not be confined to an explanation of routine procedures
    B. a manual may prove to be unsuitable for some of its anticipated uses
    C. individual messages or bulletins are more likely to be of use than are manuals
    D. a manual suffers from certain limitations that are not found in individual messages or bulletins

13. As the supervisor of a unit in an agency, you have just been instructed to put into effect a new procedure which you know will be disliked by your subordinates. 13.____
Of the following, the MOST important reason for calling a meeting of your staff before putting the new procedure into effect is to
    A. help you to determine which workers will be reluctant to cooperate in carrying out the new procedure
    B. allow you to announce that the new procedure must be put into effect despite any objections which might be raised
    C. enable you to explain that you don't approve of the new procedure and to give the reasons why it must nevertheless be put into effect
    D. permit you to discuss the purpose of the new procedure and to present the reasons for its adoption

14. Assume that you are a training conference leader and that you have just begun a series of conferences on supervisory techniques for new supervisors. Each conference is scheduled to last for three hours. A thorough discussion of all the material planned for the first session, which you had estimated would last until 4 P.M., is completed by 3:30 P.M. 14.____
For you to summarize the points that have been made and close the meeting would be
    A. *advisable*; the participants will lose interest in the conference if it is permitted to continue merely to occupy the remaining time
    B. *inadvisable*; the participants should be asked if there are any other topics that they would like to discuss
    C. *advisable*; the participants in a training conference should not be kept from their regular work for long periods of time
    D. *inadvisable*; material scheduled for discussion at future sessions should be used for the remainder of this session

15. In any agency, the top administrative officials are concerned largely with the work of overall creative planning with respect to the anticipated progress of the agency. The first-line supervisors, on the other hand, are concerned largely with the control of current action for the execution of current jobs. 15.____
On the basis of this quotation, a first-line supervisor would be CHIEFLY responsible for

A. increasing or decreasing the responsibilities of his unit to reflect changes in the policies of the agency
B. modifying the work assignments of his present staff to handle a seasonal variation in the activities of the unit
C. revising the procedure that is used for transmitting instructions from the head of the agency to the unit heads
D. raising and lowering the production goals of his unit as often as necessary to adjust them to the abilities of his subordinates

16. The control of clerical work in an agency appears impossible if the clerical work is regarded merely as a series of duties unrelated to the functions of the agency. However, this control becomes feasible when it is realized that clerical work links and coordinates the functions of the agency. 16.____
On the basis of this quotation, the MOST accurate of the following statements is that the
A. complexity of clerical work may not be fully understood by those assigned to control it
B. clerical work can be readily controlled if it is coordinated by other work of the agency
C. number of clerical tasks may be reduced by regarding coordination as the function of clerical work
D. purposes of clerical work must be understood to make possible its proper control

17. Assume that as supervisor of a unit you are to prepare a vacation schedule for the employees in your unit. 17.____
Of the following, the factor which is LEAST important for you to consider in setting up this schedule is
A. the vacation preferences of each employee in the unit
B. the anticipated workload in the unit during the vacation period
C. how well each employee has performed his work
D. how essential a specific employee's services will be during the vacation period

18. In order to promote efficiency and economy in an agency, it is advisable for the management systematize and standardize procedures and relationships insofar as this can be done; however, excessive routinizing which does not permit individual contributions or achievements should be avoided. 18.____
On the basis of this quotation, it is MOST accurate to state that
A. systematized procedures should be designed mainly to encourage individual achievements
B. standardized procedures should allow for individual accomplishments
C. systematization of procedures may not be possible in organizations which have a large variety of functions
D. individual employees of an organization must fully accept standardized procedures if the procedures are to be effective

19. Trained employees work most efficiently and with a minimum expenditure of time and energy. Suitable equipment and definite, well-developed procedures are effective only when employees know how to use the equipment and procedures. 19.____
This quotation means MOST NEARLY that
   A. employees can be trained most efficiently when suitable equipment and definite procedures are used
   B. training of employees is a costly but worthwhile investment
   C. suitable equipment and definite procedures are of greatest value when employees have been properly traced to use them
   D. the cost of suitable equipment and definite procedures is negligible when the saving in time and energy that they bring is considered

20. Assume that your supervisor has asked you to present to him comprehensive, periodic reports on the progress that your unit is making in meeting its work goals. 20.____
For you to give your superior oral reports rather than written ones is
   A. *desirable*; it will be easier for him to transmit your oral reports to his superiors
   B. *undesirable*; the oral reports will provide no permanent record to which he may refer
   C. *undesirable*; there will be less opportunity for you to discuss the oral reports with him than the written ones
   D. *desirable*; the oral reports will require little time and effort to prepare

21. Assume that an employee under your supervision complains to you that your evaluation of his work is too low. 21.____
The MOST appropriate action for you to take FIRST is to
   A. explain how you arrived at the evaluation of his work
   B. encourage him to improve the quality of his work by pointing out specifically how he can do so
   C. suggest that he appeal to an impartial higher authority if he disagrees with your evaluation
   D. point out to him specific instances in which his work has been unsatisfactory

22. The nature of the experience and education that are made a prerequisite to employment determines in large degree the training job to be done after employment begins. 22.____
On the basis of this quotation, it is MOST accurate to state that
   A. the more comprehensive the experience and education required for employment, the more extensive the training that is usually given after appointment
   B. the training that is given to employees depends upon the experience and education required of them before appointment
   C. employees who possess the experience and education required for employment should need little additional training after appointment
   D. the nature of the work that employees are expected to perform determines the training that they will need

23. Assume that you are preparing a report evaluating the work of a clerk who was transferred to your unit from another unit in the agency about a year ago. Of the following, the method that would probably be MOST helpful to you in making this evaluation is to 23.____
    A. consult the evaluations this employee received from his former supervisors
    B. observe this employee at his work for a week shortly before you prepare the report
    C. examine the employee's production records and compare them with the standards set for the position
    D. obtain tactfully from his fellow employees their frank opinions of his work

24. Of the following, the CHIEF value of a flow of work chart to the management of an organization is its usefulness in 24.____
    A. locating the causes of delay in carrying out an operation
    B. training new employees in the performance of their duties
    C. determining the effectiveness of the employees in the organization
    D. determining the accuracy of its organization chart

25. Assume that a procedure for handling certain office forms has just been extensively revised. As supervisor of a small unit, you are to instruct your subordinates in the use of the new procedure, which is rather complicated. Of the following, it would be LEAST helpful to your subordinates for you to 25.____
    A. compare the revised procedure with the one it has replaced
    B. state that you believe the revised procedure to be better than the one it has replaced
    C. tell them that they will probably find it difficult to learn the new procedure
    D. give only a general outline of the revised procedure at first and then follow with more detailed instructions

KEY (CORRECT ANSWERS)

1. A
2. D
3. D
4. B
5. C

6. B
7. A
8. C
9. D
10. C

11. B
12. B
13. D
14. A
15. B

16. B
17. C
18. B
19. C
20. B

21. A
22. B
23. C
24. A
25. C

TEST 3

DIRECTIONS: Each question or incomplete statement is followed by several suggested answers or completions. Select the one that BEST answers the question or completes the statement. *PRINT THE LETTER OF THE CORRECT ANSWER IN THE SPACE AT THE RIGHT.*

1. A methods improvement program might be called a war against habit. 1.____
The MOST accurate implication of this statement is that
   A. routine handling of routine office assignments should be discouraged
   B. standardization of office procedures may encourage employees to form inefficient work habits
   C. employees tend to continue the use of existing procedures, even when such procedures are inefficient
   D. procedures should be changed consistently to prevent them from becoming habits

2. An office supervisor may give either a written or an oral order to his subordinates when making an assignment. 2.____
Of the following, it would be MOST appropriate for a supervisor to issue an order in writing when
   A. a large number of two-page reports must be stapled together before the end of the day
   B. the assignment is to be completed within two hours after it is issued to his subordinates
   C. his subordinates have completed an identical assignment the day before
   D. several entries must be made on a form at varying intervals of time by different clerks

3. A supervisor should always remember that the instruction or training of new employees is most effective if it is given when and where it is needed. 3.____
On the basis of this quotation, it is MOST appropriate to conclude that
   A. the new employee should be trained to handle any aspect of his work at the time he starts his job
   B. the new employee should be given the training essential to get him started and additional training when he requires it
   C. an employee who has received excessive training will be just as ineffective as one who has received inadequate training
   D. a new employee is trained most effectively by his own supervisor

4. A supervisor may make assignments to his subordinates in the form of a command, a request, or a call for volunteers. 4.____
It is LEAST desirable for a supervisor to make an assignment in the form of a command when
   A. a serious emergency has risen
   B. an employee objects to carrying out an assignment
   C. the assignment must be completed immediately
   D. the assignment is an unpleasant one

5. For an office supervisor to confer periodically with his subordinates in order to anticipate job problems which are likely to arise is desirable MAINLY because 5.____
   A. there will be fewer problems for which hasty decisions will have to be made
   B. some problems which are anticipated may not arise
   C. his subordinates will learn to refer the problems arising in the unit to him
   D. constant anticipation of future problems tends to raise additional problems

6. As the supervisor of a staff of clerical employees performing various types of work, you are responsible for the accuracy and efficiency with which their work is performed. 6.____
   Of the following actions you may take to insure the accuracy of their work, the MOST practical one is for you to
   A. review each operation completed by a staff member before permitting the employee to proceed to the next operation
   B. keep a record of every error made by an employee and use this record to determine whether a careless employee should be transferred or discharged
   C. assign work in such a way that every operation is performed independently by two employees
   D. determine what errors are likely to occur and set up safeguards to prevent the occurrence of these errors

7. One of your subordinates has violated a staff regulation by failing to inform you that he will be absent on a certain day. 7.____
   Of the following, the MOST appropriate action for you to take FIRST is to
   A. discuss this matter with your immediate superior
   B. find out the reason for his failure to obey this staff regulation
   C. determine what disciplinary action other supervisors have taken in similar cases
   D. take no action if his absence did not interfere with the work of the unit; reprimand him if it did

8. A newly appointed clerk is assigned to a unit of an agency at a time when the supervisor of the unit is very busy and has little time to devote to instructing the new employee in the work he is to perform. 8.____
   Of the following, the MOST appropriate method of training this employee is for the supervisor to
   A. instruct the new employee to observe several experienced clerks at work and question them regarding any aspect of the work he does not understand
   B. delegate the job of training this employee to an employee in the unit who is qualified to instruct him
   C. assign the new employee a simple task and inform him that more complex and varied duties will be given him when the supervisor is less busy
   D. have the employee spend his time reading the agency's annual reports and the laws, rules, and regulations governing its work

9. The channels of communication between the management of a bureau and its employees not only should be kept open and working, but they should also be two-way channels. 9.____
Of the following, the MOST effective method for a supervisor to use to carry out this recommendation is to
   A. arrange periodic staff meetings and individual conferences to discuss problems and procedures with his subordinates
   B. change subordinates' assignments regularly so that they will be able to see how their work is related to the objectives of the bureau
   C. issue regular instructions, both written and oral, which clearly show each subordinate's assignments
   D. encourage his subordinates to discuss personal problems with him

10. Work measurement is an essential control tool to an office supervisor. 10.____
Of the following, the LEAST important reason for using work measurement as a control tool is that work measurement
   A. may indicate training needs of his subordinates
   B. simplifies the procedures used by the supervisor's subordinates in carrying out their assignments
   C. can indicate whether the supervisor is employing more subordinates than he really needs
   D. is a basis for determining which of the supervisor's subordinates are his most efficient

11. Internal management reporting in agencies is becoming more statistical in nature. Statistics have thus become a major tool in management supervision in agencies. 11.____
Before deciding to adopt statistical reporting as a management tool, the management of an agency should FIRST determine whether the
   A. employees of the agency understand the need for, and the use of, statistics in reporting
   B. supervisory staff in the agency is capable of putting reports into statistical form
   C. major activities of the agency can be reported statistically
   D. present achievements of the agency can be compared statistically with those of previous years

12. When assigning work, which of the following criteria would be BEST for a supervisor to use? 12.____
   A. Allow each employee to select the tasks he or she does best
   B. Assign all unimportant work to the slower employees
   C. Assign the more tiring tasks to the newer employees
   D. Assign tasks based on the abilities of employees

13. You have been supervising ten people for sixteen months. During that time, your employees have never reported any problems to you. 13.____
It is LIKELY that
   A. you are doing such a good job there is no room for improvement

B. since your staff is small, the chances of problems arising are smaller than in a larger unit
C. for some reason your staff is reluctant to discuss problems with you
D. your employees are very competent and are handling all of the problems well by themselves

14. Your supervisor informs you that three of your fifteen employees have complained to her about your inconsistent methods of supervision. 14.____
You should
A. offer to attend a supervisory training program
B. first ask her if it is proper for her to allow these employees to go over your head
C. ask her what specific acts have been considered inconsistent
D. explain that you have purposely been inconsistent because of the needs of these three employees

15. On short notice, a supervisor must ask her staff to work overtime. 15.____
Of the following, it would be BEST to
A. explain they would be doing her a personal favor which she would appreciate a great deal
B. explain why it is necessary
C. reassure them that they can take the time off in the near future
D. remind them that working overtime occasionally is part of the job requirement

16. One of your employees has begun reporting to work late on the average of twice a week. 16.____
You should
A. send a memo to everyone in your unit, stressing that lateness cannot be tolerated
B. privately discuss the matter with the employee to determine if there are any unusual circumstances causing the behavior
C. bring the issue up at the next staff meeting, without singling out any employee
D. ask one of your employees to discuss the matter with the individual

17. One of your employees submitted an application for acceptance into a career development workshop two months ago and has heard nothing. The individual tells you that when one of her co-workers submitted an application, he received a reply a week later. 17.____
Which is the BEST response for you to make?
A. This is obviously a case of discrimination. I'll bring it to the Affirmative Action officer immediately.
B. Next time you submit a request for something of this nature, let me know and I will write a cover letter that will carry more weight.
C. Perhaps it was an oversight. Why don't you call the organization and ask why you've heard nothing?
D. it looks like you won't be accepted this year. Be sure to try again next year.

18. In order to meet deadlines, a supervisor should 18.____
    A. schedule the work and keep informed of its progress
    B. delegate work
    C. hire temporary personnel
    D. know the capabilities of his or her most reliable employees

19. Your supervisor has given instructions to your employees in your absence that differ from those you had given them. 19.____
    You should
    A. have your employees follow your instructions
    B. have your employees follow your supervisor's instructions
    C. discuss the matter with your supervisor
    D. discuss the matter with your employees and find out which method they think is best

20. You have found it necessary to return an assignment completed by one of your employees so that several changes can be made. The employee objects to making these changes. 20.____
    The MOST appropriate action for you to take FIRST is to
    A. inform the employee that he or she is free to object to your supervisor
    B. ask if the employee has carefully read your proposed changes
    C. calmly state that your decision is final, and further discussion will most likely be useless
    D. allow the employee to present his or her objections against making the changes

21. Among the problems that confront a new supervisor in relation to her or his employees, the one which requires the MOST unusual degree of skill and diplomacy is 21.____
    A. changing established ideas
    B. calling attention to mistakes
    C. gaining the respect of employees
    D. training new employees

22. Of the following, the BEST indication of high morale in a supervisor's unit would be the 22.____
    A. unit never has to work overtime
    B. supervisor often enjoys staying late to plan work for the following day
    C. unit gives expensive birthday presents to each other
    D. employees are willing to give first priority to attaining group objectives, subordinating personal desires they may have

23. In the satisfactory handling of an employee's complaint which is fancied rather than real, the complaint should be considered 23.____
    A. not very important since it has no basis in fact
    B. as important as a grievance grounded in fact
    C. an attempt by the employee to create trouble
    D. an indication of a psychological problem on the part of the employee

24. You are attempting to teach a new employee in your unit how to change a typewriter ribbon. The employee is having a great deal of difficulty changing the ribbon, even though you have always found it simple to do. 24.____
Before you spend more time instructing the individual, you should
    A. ask if the employee working nearest would take responsibility for changing the ribbon in the future
    B. tell the employee that you never found this difficult and ask what he or she finds difficult about it
    C. review each of the steps you have already explained and determine whether the individual understands them
    D. tell the employee that you will continue after lunch because you are getting irritable

25. One of your workers has relatives who raise chickens. One day, you mention in casual conversation that you bought some eggs of poor quality at the grocery store. The following Monday, the worker places a box of fresh eggs on your desk. You thank him and offer to pay, but he refuses. On several occasions thereafter, he brings in additional eggs but still refuses to take payment. He is obviously proud of these products and seems to take great pleasure in sharing them with you. However, you begin to hear rumors that the other workers believe that you and the worker are very friendly and that he is receiving special privileges from you. 25.____
You should
    A. explain the situation to the worker, pointing out that he is being hurt by the conditions because of the feelings of others
    B. ignore the situation since the worker is merely being friendly and is actually receiving no favors in return
    C. supervise this worker more carefully than the others to insure that he will not take advantage of the situation
    D. refuse all gifts from the worker thereafter without further explanation

KEY (CORRECT ANSWERS)

1. C
2. D
3. B
4. D
5. A

6. D
7. B
8. B
9. A
10. B

11. C
12. D
13. C
14. C
15. B

16. B
17. C
18. A
19. C
20. D

21. A
22. D
23. B
24. C
25. A

TEST 4

DIRECTIONS: Each question or incomplete statement is followed by several suggested answers or completions. Select the one that BEST answers the question or completes the statement. *PRINT THE LETTER OF THE CORRECT ANSWER IN THE SPACE AT THE RIGHT.*

1. Lax supervision has been blamed largely on the unwillingness of supervisors to supervise their employees. 1.____
The CHIEF reason for this unwillingness to supervise is based MAINLY on the supervisors'
   A. failure to accept modern concepts of proper supervision
   B. doubt of their ability to keep pace with modern techniques and developments in supervision
   C. fear of complaints from employees and the supervisors' wish to avoid unpleasantness
   D. inability to adhere to the same high standards of performance which are required of employees

2. The appraisal of employees and their performance is an integral part of the supervisor's job. There is wide agreement that several basic principles must be taken into account by supervisors involved in the appraisal process in order to perform this function correctly. 2.____
The one of the statements below that LEAST represents a basic principle of the appraisal process is:
   A. Appraisals should be based more on performance of definite tasks than on personality considerations.
   B. Appraisal of long-range potential should rely heavily on subjective judgment of that potential.
   C. Appraisal involves the use of value judgments by the supervisor and does, therefore, require reference to pre-established standards.
   D. Appraisal should aim at emphasizing employees' strengths rather than weaknesses.

3. Although accuracy and speed are both important in the performance of work, accuracy should be considered more important MAINLY because 3.____
   A. most supervisors insist on accurate work
   B. much time is lost in correcting errors
   C. a rapid rate of work cannot be maintained for any length of time
   D. speedy workers are often inaccurate

4. If an employee has done a complicated task well, his or her supervisor should 4.____
   A. tell the employee that he or she has done a good job
   B. call a staff meeting to see if anyone has suggestions for improving future performance of the task
   C. avoid commending the employee as performing competently is what they are paid to do
   D. confide in the employee that he or she is the best worker in your unit

5. You are a newly appointed supervisor in a large office. It had been the practice in that office for the employees to take an unauthorized coffee break at 10:00 A.M. You have been successful in stopping this practice, and for one week no one had gone out for coffee at 10:00 A.M. One day, a stenographer comes over to you at 10:15 A.M., appearing to be ill. She states that she doesn't feel well and that she would like to go out for a cup of tea. She asks your permission to leave the office for a few minutes. 5.____
You should
   A. telephone and have a cup of tea delivered to her
   B. permit her to go out
   C. refuse her permission, explaining that you don't wish to set a bad example
   D. tell her she can leave for an early lunch

6. One of the employees you supervise has just put up a small poster in her work area that two of your eight employees find obscene and distasteful. While you don't like the poster either, it doesn't upset you. The two employees already have complained to you about the poster. 6.____
Of the following, you should
   A. have the two employees talk to the individual and explain why they are offended
   B. privately explain to the individual that her poster is causing some problems and seek her cooperation in removing it
   C. do nothing as the employee has the right to express her feelings
   D. compromise and allow her to display the poster half of the time

7. One of the most effective ways to build a sense of employee pride, teamwork, and motivation is for the supervisor to seek advice, suggestions, and information from employees concerning ways in which work should be solved. Many experiments in group decision-making have indicated that work groups can help the supervisor in improving decision-making. Where employees feel that they are really part of a team and that they have a significant influence on the decisions that are made, they are more likely to accept the decisions and to seek new solutions to future difficult problems. 7.____
According to the above passage, a supervisor should
   A. almost always follow the advice of his or her employees in handling difficult problems
   B. always seek advice from employees when handling difficult problems
   C. choices A and D, but not B
   D. look to employees for assistance in decision-making

8. You have just had a private discussion with the employee with the poster in Question 6 above. You have explained that her poster is causing some problems, and have asked for her cooperation in removing it. She has politely refused to do so, saying, "looking at it cheers her up, and she's been depressed lately." 8.____
You should
   A. wait a day or two to see if the incident blows over before deciding whether to take any further action

B. call in the two disgruntled employees within the hour and let them know they'll have to live with the poster as you are not going to act as a censor in the office
C. check agency policies to see if it is legal to have posters down as it is interfering with the work of the unit

9. An employee reprimanded for poor performance tells her supervisor that her recent behavior has been due to a serious family problem. The supervisor suggests several programs which may be able to help her. 9.____
The action of the supervisor was
A. *inappropriate*; the supervisor should not involve herself in the personal affairs of her subordinates
B. *appropriate*; personal problems frequently affect job performance
C. *inappropriate*; the employee may consider the supervisor responsible for the subsequent action of the social agencies
D. *appropriate*; the discussion with the supervisor will in itself tend to solve the problem

10. Your supervisor informs you that the employee turnover rate in your office is well above the norm and must be reduced. 10.____
Which one of the following initial steps would be LEAST appropriate in attempting to overcome this problem?
A. Decide to be more lenient about the performance standards and about employee requests for time off, so that your office will gain a reputation as a good place to work.
B. Discuss the problem with a few of your employees whose judgment you trust to see if they can provide insight into the underlying causes of the problem.
C. Review the records of employees who have left during the past year to see if they can shed some light on the underlying causes of the problem.
D. Carefully review your training procedures to see if they can be improved

11. The management principle that each employee should be under the direct control of one immediate supervisor at any one time is known as the principle of 11.____
A. chain of command
B. span of control
C. unity of command
D. homogeneous assignment

12. The employees of a unit have been wasteful in the use of office supplies. 12.____
Of the following, the MOST desirable action for the supervisor to take to reduce this waste is to
A. determine the average quantity of supplies used daily by each employee
B. find out which employees have been most wasteful and reprimand those employees
C. discuss this matter at a conference with the staff, pointing out the necessity for, and methods of, eliminating waste
D. issue supplies for an assignment at the time the assignment is made and limit the quantity to the amount needed for that assignment only

13. You supervise nineteen employees in a unit which is located directly across from the commissioner's office. One of your new employees has a habit of *showing off* whenever the commissioner is nearby. You have just heard other employees laughing about this behavior among themselves. You like the new employee and would like the employee to be accepted by the others. Of the following, you should 13.____
    A. discuss the situation with two of the older employees and seek their cooperation in being a little more tolerant
    B. talk with the new employee and gently explain the situation
    C. discuss the situation with your most trusted employees and ask them to talk to the others
    D. do nothing

14. One of your employees comes to you and complains of sexual harassment by your supervisor. The employee has frequently complained about minor issues in the six months she's been there. You have known your supervisor for thirteen years and respect him a great deal. You have known your supervisor for thirteen years and respect him a great deal. Of the following, you should 14.____
    A. firmly let the employee know what a serious allegation she is bringing against your supervisor
    B. let the employee know you will take her concerns seriously
    C. call your supervisor and give him a chance to prepare a defense
    D. inform the employee that she had better have concrete proof for a charge of this nature

15. The one of the following which is usually the POOREST reason for transferring an employee is to 15.____
    A. grant a doctor's request that the employee work nearer to his or her home
    B. take care of changes in workload
    C. relieve the monotony of work assignments

16. You find that you have unjustly reprimanded one of your subordinates. You should 16.____
    A. ignore the matter, but be more careful in the future
    B. readily admit your mistake to the employee
    C. admit your mistake at your next staff meeting so that your employees will know how fair you are
    D. admit your mistake, but blame the misunderstanding on your supervisor

17. An experienced, self-confident employee carelessly omitted an essential operation on a job assigned to her. As a result, the completion of an important urgent report was delayed for several hours. A few days later, a relatively inexperienced, sensitive co-worker made a similar careless mistake with similar negative results. The supervisor of the two employees was more gentle in reprimanding the latter than the former employee. 17.____

The supervisor's action in administering reprimands of unequal severity to these two subordinates was

A. *not appropriate*, because fairness requires that subordinates responsible for like mistakes receive reprimands of like severity
B. *appropriate*, because supervisors should consider the temperament of subordinates when reprimanding them
C. *appropriate*, because subordinates who accept greater responsibilities must likewise accept the consequent greater penalties for their mistakes
D. *not appropriate*, because more experienced employees benefit less, in general, from reprimands than less experienced employees

18. You have just overheard a tense discussion in the cafeteria between two of your best employees. One of them has owed the other $40 for several months and has not paid it back or even mentioned the debt. The employees do not realize that you have heard them. 18.____
During that week, you should

A. not discuss the matter with either of them
B. discuss the matter with both of them, as the conflict may adversely affect their job performance
C. discuss the matter with the one who has not paid back the money
D. put a clever but meaningful cartoon up on your wall about the importance of paying back debts to friends

19. You have been supervising twenty employees for three months. You suspect that one of your employees, who has worked in the unit longer than anyone else, has perfected the art of looking busy. You wish to find out how much work she is really accomplishing. 19.____
Of the following, it would be LEAST appropriate to

A. have a frank discussion with the employee about her performance
B. set specific time limits on when you would like to get work back from her
C. try to observe her more carefully while she is working
D. be more careful when monitoring her work output

20. The supervisor of a central files bureau which has fifty employees customarily spends a considerable portion of time in spot-checking the files, reviewing material being transferred from active to inactive files, and similar activities. 20.____
From the viewpoint of the department management, the MOST pertinent evaluation which can be made on the basis of this information is that the

A. supervisor is conscientious and hardworking
B. bureau may need additional staff
C. supervisor has not made a sufficient delegation of authority and responsibility
D. bureau needs an in-service training course as the work of its employees requires an abnormal amount of review

21. You have just been appointed as supervisor of ten employees. The supervisor you are replacing demanded that her subordinate accept their assignments without question. She refused to allow them to exercise initiative in carrying out assignments and maintained a constant check on their work performance. 21.____

The MOST appropriate policy for you to adopt would be to
- A. gradually remove the controls you consider too strict and provide opportunities for your staff to participate in formulating work plans and procedures
- B. continue her rigid policies, as the employees are used to this
- C. discontinue all strict controls immediately and give the employees complete freedom in carrying out their assignments
- D. ask your employees what method of supervision they would prefer

22. In any agency, the top administrative officials are concerned largely with the work of overall creative planning with respect to the anticipated progress of the agency. The first-line supervisors, on the other hand, are concerned largely with the control of current action for the execution of current jobs. On the basis of this quotation, a first-line supervisor would be CHIEFLY responsible for 22.____
    - A. increasing or decreasing the responsibilities of his or her unit to reflect changes in the policies of the agency
    - B. modifying the work assignments of his or her present staff to handle a seasonal variation in the activities of the unit
    - C. revising the procedure that is used for transmitting instructions from the head of the agency to the unit heads
    - D. raising and lowering the production goals of his or her unit as often as necessary to adjust them to the abilities of employees

23. As a supervisor, you may find it necessary to consult with your superior before taking action on some matters. 23.____
    Of the following, the action for which it is MOST important that you obtain the prior approval of your superior is one that involves
    - A. assuming additional functions for your unit
    - B. rotating assignments among your staff members
    - C. initiating regular meetings of your staff
    - D. assigning certain members of your staff to work overtime on an emergency job

24. Suppose that a clerk who is employed in a unit under your supervision performs his work quickly but carelessly. He is about to be transferred to another unit in your department. The chief of this other unit asks you for your opinion of this employee's work habits. The chief of this other unit asks you for your opinion of this employee's work habits. 24.____
    Of the following, the MOST appropriate reply for you to make is to
    - A. point out this employee's good qualities only since he may correct his bad qualities after his transfer is effected
    - B. say nothing good or bad about this employee, thus permitting him to start his new assignment with a clean slate
    - C. inform the unit chief that this clerk performed his work speedily but was careless
    - D. emphasize his employee's good points and minimize his bad points

25. Of the following, the action that is likely to contribute MOST to the prestige of a supervisor is for him to 25.____
   A. expect al his subordinates to perform with equal efficiency any tasks assigned to them
   B. observe the same rules of conduct that he expects his subordinates to observe
   C. seek their advice on his personal problems and offer them his advice on their personal problems
   D. be always frank and outspoken to his subordinates in pointing out their faults

KEY (CORRECT ANSWERS)

1. C
2. B
3. B
4. A
5. B

6. B
7. D
8. A
9. B
10. A

11. C
12. C
13. D
14. B
15. D

16. B
17. B
18. A
19. A
20. C

21. A
22. B
23. A
24. C
25. C

EXAMINATION SECTION

TEST 1

DIRECTIONS: Each question or incomplete statement is followed by several suggested answers or completions. Select the one that BEST answers the question or completes the statement. *PRINT THE LETTER OF THE CORRECT ANSWER IN THE SPACE AT THE RIGHT.*

1. When a supervisor in a large office introduces a change in the regular office procedure, it is USUAL to expect 1.____
   A. immediate acceptance by office staff, unless the change is unnecessary
   B. an immediate production increase, since new procedures are more stimulating than old ones
   C. a temporary production loss, even if the change is really an overall improvement
   D. resistance to the change only if it has been put into writing

2. A supervisor evaluates the performance of subordinates and then applies measures, where needed, which result in bringing performance up to desired standards. 2.____
   Which of the following functions of management might he BEST be described as performing?
   A. Organizing B. Controlling C. Directing D. Planning

3. Assume that, as a supervisor, you have been assigned responsibility for a new and complex project which entails collection and analysis of data. You have prepared general written instructions which explain the project and procedures to be followed by several statisticians. 3.____
   Which of the following procedures would be MOST advisable for you, as the supervisor, to follow?
   A. Distribute the instructions to your subordinates to come to you with any important questions
   B. Distribute the instructions and advise subordinates to come to you with any important questions
   C. Meet with subordinates as a group and explain the project using the written instructions as a handout
   D. Delegate responsibility for further explanation of the project to an immediate qualified subordinate to free you for concentration on research design

4. Supervisors have an obligation to make careful and thorough appraisals and reports of probationary employees. 4.____
   Of the following, the MOST important justification for this statement is that the probationary period
   A. should be used for positive development of the employee's understanding of the organization
   B. is the most effective period for changing a new employee's knowledges, skills, and attitudes

C. insures that the employee will meet work standard requirements on future assignments
D. should be considered as the final step in the selection process

5. Many studies of management indicate that a principal reason for failure of supervisors lies in their ability to delegate duties effectively. 5.____
Which one of the following practices by a supervisor would NOT be a block to successful delegation?
A. Instructing the delegate to follow a set procedure in carrying out the assignment
B. Maintaining point-by-point control over the process delegated
C. Transferring ultimate responsibility for the duties assigned to the delegate
D. Requiring the delegate to keep the delegator informed of his progress

6. Crosswise communication occurs between personnel at lower or middle levels of different organizational units. It often speeds information and improves understanding, but has certain dangers. 6.____
Of the following proposed policies, which would NOT be important as a safeguard in crosswise communication?
A. Supervisors should agree as to how crosswise communication should occur.
B. Crosswise relationships must exist only between employees of equal status.
C. Subordinates must keep their superiors informed about their interdepartmental communications.
D. Subordinates must refrain from making commitments beyond their authority.

7. Systems theory has given us certain principles which are as applicable to organizational and social activities as they are to those of science. 7.____
With regard to the training of employees in an organization, which of the following is likely to be MOST consistent with the modern systems approach?
Training can be effective ONLY when it is
A. related to the individual abilities of the employees
B. done on all levels of the organizational hierarchy
C. evaluated on the basis of experimental and control groups
D. provided on the job by the immediate supervisor

8. The management of a large agency, before making a decision as to whether or not to computerize its operations, should have a feasibility study made. 8.____
Of the following, the one which is LEAST important to include in such a study is
A. the current abilities of management and staff to use a computer
B. projected workloads and changes in objectives of functional units in the agency
C. the contributions expected of each organizational unit towards achievement of agency objectives
D. the decision-making activity and informational needs of each management function

9. Managing information covers the creation, collection, processing, storage, and transmission of information that appears in a variety of forms. A supervisor responsible for a statistical unit can be considered, in many respects, an information manager.
Of the following, which would be considered the LEAST important aspect of the information manager's job? 9.____
   A. Establishing better information standards and forms
   B. Reducing the amount of unnecessary paperwork performed
   C. Producing progressively greater numbers of informational reports
   D. Developing a greater appreciation for information among management members

10. Because of the need for improvement in information systems throughout industry and government, various techniques for improving these systems have been developed.
Of these, *systems simulation* is a technique for improving systems which 10.____
   A. creates new ideas and concepts through the use of a computer
   B. deals with time controlling of interrelated systems which make up an overall project
   C. permits experimentation with various ideas to see what results might be obtained
   D. does not rely on assumptions which condition the value of the results

11. The one of the following which it is NOT advisable for a supervisor to do when dealing with individual employees is to 11.____
   A. recognize a person's outstanding service as well as his mistakes
   B. help an employee satisfy his need to excel
   C. encourage an efficient employee to seek better opportunities even if this action may cause the supervisor to lose a good worker
   D. take public notice of an employee's mistakes so that fewer errors will be made in the future

12. Suppose that you are in a department where you are given the responsibility for teaching seven new assistants a number of routine procedures that all assistants should know.
Of the following, the BEST method for you to follow in teaching these procedures is to 12.____
   A. separate the slower learners from the faster learners and adapt your presentation to their level of ability
   B. instruct all the new employees in a group without attempting to assess differences in learning rates
   C. restrict your approach to giving them detailed written instructions in order to save time
   D. avoid giving the employees written instructions in order to force them to memorize job procedures quickly

13. Suppose that you are a supervisor to whom several assistants must hand in work for review. You notice that one of the assistants gets very upset whenever you discover an error in his work, although all the assistants make mistakes from time to time. 13.____
Of the following, it would be BEST for you to
   A. arrange discreetly for the employee's work to be reviewed by another supervisor
   B. ignore his reaction since giving attention to such behavior increases its intensity
   C. suggest that the employee seek medical help since he has such great difficulty in accepting normal criticism
   D. try to build the employee's self-confidence by emphasizing those parts of his work that are done well

14. Suppose you are a supervisor responsible for supervising a number of assistants in an agency where each assistant receives a manual of policies and procedures when he first reports for work. You have been asked to teach your subordinates a new procedure which requires knowledge of several items of policy and procedure found in the manual. 14.____
The one of the following techniques which it would be BEST for you to employ is to
   A. give verbal instructions which include a review of the appropriate standard procedures as well as an explanation of new tasks
   B. give individual instruction restricted to the new procedure to each assistant as the need arises
   C. provide written instructions for new procedural elements and refer employees to their manuals for explanation of standard procedures
   D. ask employees to review appropriate sections of their manual and then explain those aspects of the new procedure which the manual did not cover

15. Supposes that you are a supervisor in charge of a unit in which changes in work procedures are about to be instituted. 15.____
The one of the following which you, as the supervisor, should anticipate as being MOST likely to occur during the changeover is
   A. a temporary rise in production because of interest in the new procedures
   B. uniform acceptance of these procedures on the part of your staff
   C. varying interpretations of the new procedures by your staff
   D. general agreement among staff members that the new procedures are advantageous

16. Suppose that a supervisor and one of the assistants under his supervision are known to be friends who play golf together on weekends. 16.____
The maintenance of such a friendship on the part of the supervisor is GENERALLY
   A. *acceptable* as long as this assistant continues to perform his duties satisfactorily
   B. *unacceptable* since the supervisor will find it difficult to treat the assistant as a subordinate

C. *acceptable* if the supervisor does not favor this assistant above other employees
D. *unacceptable* because the other assistants will resent the friendship regardless of the supervisor's behavior on the job

17. Suppose that you are a supervisor assigned to review the financial records of an agency which has recently undergone a major reorganization. Which of the following would it be BEST for you to do FIRST? 17.____
    A. Interview the individual in charge of agency financial operations to determine whether the organizational changes affect the system of financial review
    B. Discuss the nature of the reorganization with your own supervisor to anticipate and plan a new financial review procedure
    C. Carry out the financial review as usual, and adjust your methods to any problems arising from the reorganization
    D. Request a written report from the agency head explaining the nature of the reorganization and recommending changes in the system of financial review

18. Suppose that a newly assigned supervisor finds that he must delegate some of his duties to subordinates in order to get the work done. Which one of the following would NOT be a block to his delegating these duties effectively? 18.____
    A. Inability to give proper directions as to what he wants done
    B. Reluctance to take calculated risks
    C. Lack of trust in his subordinates
    D. Retaining ultimate responsibility for the delegated work

19. A supervisor sometimes performs the staff function of preparing and circulating reports among bureau chiefs. Which of the following is LEAST important as an objective in designing and writing such reports? 19.____
    A. Providing relevant information on past, present, and future actions
    B. Modifying his language in order to insure goodwill among the bureau chiefs
    C. Helping the readers of the report to make appropriate decisions
    D. Summarizing important information to help readers see trends or outstanding points

20. Suppose you are a supervisor assigned to prepare a report to be read by all bureau chiefs in your agency. The MOST important reason for avoiding highly technical accounting terminology in writing this report is to 20.____
    A. ensure the accuracy and relevancy of the text
    B. insure winning the readers' cooperation
    C. make the report more interesting to the readers
    D. make it easier for the readers to understand

21. Which of the following conditions is MOST likely to cause low morale in an office? 21.____
    A. Different standards of performance for individuals in the same title
    B. A requirement that employees perform at full capacity
    C. Standards of performance that vary with titles of employees
    D. Careful attention to the image of the division or department

22. A wise supervisor or representative of management realizes that, in the relationship between supervisor and subordinates, all power is not on the side of management, and that subordinates do sometimes react to restrictive authority in such a manner as to seriously retard management's objectives. A wise supervisor does not stimulate such reactions. 22.____
    In the subordinate's attempt to retaliate against an unusually authoritative management style, which of the following actions would generally be LEAST successful for the subordinate? He
    A. joins with other employees in organizations to deal with management
    B. obviously delays in carrying out instructions which are given in an arrogant or incisive manner
    C. performs assignments exactly as instructed even when he recognizes errors in instructions
    D. holds back the flow of feedback information to superiors

23. Which of the following is the MOST likely and costly effect of vague and indefinite instructions given to subordinates by a supervisor? 23.____
    A. Misunderstanding and ineffective work on the part of the subordinates
    B. A necessity for the supervisor to report identical instructions with each assignment
    C. A failure of the supervisor to adequately keep the attention of subordinates
    D. Inability of subordinates to assist each other in the absence of the supervisor

24. At the professional level, there is a kind of informal authority which exercises itself even though no delegation of authority has taken place from higher management. It occurs within the context of knowledge required and professional competence in a special area. 24.____
    An example of the kind of authority described in this statement is MOST clearly exemplified in the situation where a senior supervisor influences associates and subordinates by virtue of the
    A. salary level fixed for his particular set of duties
    B. amount of college training he possesses
    C. technical position he has gained and holds on the work team
    D. initiative and judgment he has demonstrated to his supervisor

25. An assistant under your supervision attempts to conceal the fact that he has made an error. 25.____
    Under this circumstance, it would be BEST for you, as the supervisor, to proceed on the assumption that

A. this evasion indicates something wrong in the fundamental relationship between you and the assistant
B. this evasion is not deliberate, if the error is subsequently corrected by the assistant
C. this evasion should be overlooked if the error is not significant
D. detection and correction of errors will come about as an automatic consequence of internal control procedures

---

KEY (CORRECT ANSWERS)

1.	C	11.	D
2.	B	12.	B
3.	C	13.	D
4.	D	14.	A
5.	D	15.	C
6.	B	16.	C
7.	B	17.	A
8.	A	18.	D
9.	C	19.	B
10.	C	20.	D

21.	A
22.	B
23.	A
24.	C
25.	A

TEST 2

DIRECTIONS: Each question or incomplete statement is followed by several suggested answers or completions. Select the one that BEST answers the question or completes the statement. *PRINT THE LETTER OF THE CORRECT ANSWER IN THE SPACE AT THE RIGHT.*

1. The unit which you supervise has a number of attorneys, accountants, examiners, statisticians, and clerks who prepare some of the routine papers required to be filed. In order to be certain that nothing goes out of your office that is improper, you have instituted a system that requires that you review and initial all moving papers, memoranda of law and briefs that are prepared. As a result, you put in a great deal of overtime and even must take work home with you frequently. 1.____
A situation such as this is
   A. inevitable if you are to keep proper controls over the quality of the office work product
   B. indicative of the fact that the agency must provide an additional position within your office for an assistant supervisor who would do all the reviewing, leaving you free for other pressing administrative work and to handle the most difficult work in your unit
   C. the logical result of an ever-increasing caseload
   D. symptomatic of poor supervision and management

2. Your unit has been assigned a new employee who has never worked for the city. 2.____
To orient him to his job in your unit, of the following, the BEST procedure is first to
   A. assign him to another employee to whatever work that employee gives him so that he can become familiar with your work and at the same time be productive
   B. give him copies of the charter and code provisions affecting your operations plus any in-office memoranda or instructions that are available and have him read them
   C. assign him to work on a relatively simple problem and then, after he has finished it, tell him politely what he did wrong
   D. explain to him the duties of his position and the functions of the office

3. A bureau chief who supervises other supervisors makes it a practice to assign them more cases than they can possibly handle. 3.____
This approach is
   A. *right*, because it results in getting more work done than would otherwise be the case
   B. *right*, because it relieves the bureau chief making the assignments of the responsibility of getting the work done
   C. *wrong*, because it builds resistance on the part of those called upon to handle the caseload
   D. *wrong*, because superiors lose track of cases

4. Assume you are a supervisor and are expected to exercise *authority* over subordinates. 4.____
Which of the following BEST defines *authority*? The
   A. ability to control the nature of the contribution a subordinate is desirous of making
   B. innate inability to get others to do for you what you want to get done irrespective of their own wishes
   C. legal right conferred by the agency to control the actions of others
   D. power to determine a subordinate's attitude toward his agency and his superiors

5. Paternalistic leadership stresses a paternal or fatherly influence in the relationships between the leader and the group and is manifest in a watchful care for the comfort and welfare of the followers. 5.____
Which one of the following statements regarding paternalistic leadership is MOST accurate?
   A. Employees who work well under paternalistic leadership come to expect such leadership even when the paternal leader has left the organization.
   B. Most disputes arising out of supervisor-subordinate relationships develop because group leaders do not understand the principles of paternalistic leadership.
   C. Paternalistic leadership frequently destroys office relationships because most employees are turned into non-thinking dependent robots.
   D. Paternalistic leadership is rarely, if ever, successful because employees resent paternalistic leadership which they equate with weakness.

6. Employees who have extensive dealings with members of the public should have, as much as possible, *real acceptance* of all people and a willingness to serve everyone impartially and objectively. 6.____
Assuming that this statement is correct, the one of the following which would be the BEST demonstration of *real acceptance* is
   A. condoning antisocial behavior
   B. giving the appearance of agreeing with everyone encountered
   C. refusing to give opinions on anyone's behavior
   D. understanding the feelings expressed through a person's behavior

7. Assume that the agency chief has requested you to help plan a public relations program because of recent complaints from citizens about the unbecoming conduct and language of various groups of city employees who have dealings with the public. 7.____
In carrying out this assignment, the one of the following steps which should be undertaken FIRST is to
   A. study the characteristics of the public clientele dealt with by employees in your agency
   B. arrange to have employees attend several seminars on human relations
   C. develop several procedures for dealing with the public and allow the staff to choose the one which is best
   D. find out whether the employees in your agency may oppose any plan proposed by you

8. The one of the following statements which BEST expresses the relationship between the morale of government employees and the public relations aspects of their work is: 8.____
   A. There is little relationship between employee morale and public relations, chiefly because public opinion is shaped primarily by response to departmental policy formulation.
   B. Employee morale is closely related to public relations, chiefly because the employee's morale will largely determine the manner in which he deals with the public.
   C. There is little relationship between employee morale and public relations, chiefly because public relations is primarily a function of the agency's public relations department.
   D. Employee morale is closely related to public relations, chiefly because employee morale indicates the attitude of the agency's top officials toward the public.

9. As a supervisor, you are required to deal extensively with the public. The agency chief has indicated that he is considering holding a special in-service training course for employees in communications skills 9.____
   Holding this training course would be
   A. *advisable*, chiefly because government employees should receive formal training in public relations skills
   B. *inadvisable*, chiefly because the public regards such training as a *waste of the taxpayers money*
   C. *advisable*, chiefly because such training will enable the employee to aid in drafting departmental press releases
   D. *inadvisable*, chiefly because of the great difficulty involved in developing skills through formal instruction

10. Assume that you have extensive contact with the public. In dealing with the public, sensitivity to an individual's attitudes is important because these attitudes can be used to predict behavior. 10.____
    However, the MAIN reason that attitudes CANNOT successfully predict all behavior is that
    A. attitudes are highly resistant to change
    B. an individual acquires attitudes as a function of growing up in a particular cultural environment
    C. attitudes are only one of many factors which determine a person's behavior
    D. an individual's behavior is not always observable

11. Rotation of employees from assignment to assignment is sometimes advocated by management experts. 11.____
    Of the following, the MOST probable advantage to the organization of this practice is that it leads to
    A. higher specialization of duties so that excessive identification with the overall organization is reduced
    B. increased loyalty of employees to their immediate supervisors

C. greater training and development of employees
D. intensified desire of employees to obtain additional, outside formal education

12. Usually, a supervisor should attempt to standardize the work for which he is responsible. 12.____
The one of the following which is a BASIC reason for doing this is to
A. eliminate the need to establish priorities
B. permit the granting of exceptions to rules and special circumstances
C. facilitate the taking of action based on applicable standards
D. learn the identity of outstanding employees

13. The differences between line and staff authority are often quite ambiguous. 13.____
Of the following, the ESSENTIAL difference is that
A. *line authority* is exercised by first-level supervisors; *staff authority* is exercised by higher-level supervisors and managerial staff
B. *staff authority* is the right to issue directives; *line authority* is entirely consultative
C. *line authority* is the power to make decisions regarding intra-agency matters; *staff authority* involves decisions regarding inter-agency matters
D. *staff authority* is largely advisory; *line authority* is the right to command

14. Modern management theory stresses work-centered motivation as one way of increasing the productivity of employees. 14.____
The one of the following which is PARTICULARLY characteristic of such motivation is that it
A. emphasizes the crucial role of routinization of procedures
B. stresses the satisfaction to be found in performing work
C. features the value of wages and fringe benefits
D. uses a firm but fair method of discipline

15. The agency's informal communications network is called the *grapevine*. 15.____
If employees are learning about important organizational developments primarily through the grapevine, this is MOST likely an indication that
A. official channels of communication are not functioning so efficiently as they should
B. supervisory personnel are making effective use of the grapevine to communicate with subordinates
C. employees already have a clear understanding of the agency's policies and procedures
D. upward formal channels of communication within the agency are informing management of employee grievances

16. Of the following, a flow chart is BEST described as a chart which shows 16.____
A. the places through which work moves in the course of the job process
B. which employees perform specific functions leading to the completion of a job

C. the schedules for production and how they eliminate waiting time between jobs
D. how work units are affected by the actions of related work units

17. Evaluation of the results of training is necessary in order to assess its value. Of the following, the BEST technique for the supervisor to use in determining whether the training under consideration actually resulted in the desired modification of the behavior of the employee concerned is through 17.____
A. inference B. job analysis C. observation D. simulation

18. The usual distinction between line and staff authority is that staff authority is mainly advisory, whereas line authority is the right to command. However, a third category has been suggested-prescriptive-to distinguish those personnel whose functions may be formally defined as staff but in practice exercise considerable authority regarding decisions relating to their specialties. 18.____
The one of the following which indicates the MAJOR purpose of creating this third category is to
A. develop the ability of each employee to perform a greater number of tasks
B. reduce line-staff conflict
C. prevent over-specialization of functions
D. encourage decision-making by line personnel

19. It is sometimes considered desirable to train employees to a standard of proficiency higher than that deemed necessary for actual job performance. 19.____
The MOST likely reason for such overtraining would be to
A. eliminate the need for standards
B. increase the value of refresher training
C. compensate for previous lack of training
D. reduce forgetting or loss of skill

20. Assume that you have been directed to immediately institute various new procedures in the handling of records. 20.____
Of the following, the BEST method for you to use to insure that your subordinates know exactly what to do is to
A. circulate a memorandum explaining the new procedure have your subordinates initial it
B. explain the new procedures to one or two subordinates and ask them to tell the others
C. have a meeting with your subordinates to give them copies of the procedures and discuss it with them
D. post the new procedures where they can be referred to by all those concerned

21. A supervisor decided to hold a problem-solving conference with his entire staff and distributed an announcement and agenda one week before the meeting. 21.____
Of the following, the BEST reason for providing each participant with an agenda is that
   A. participants will feel that something will be accomplished
   B. participants may prepare for the conference
   C. controversy will be reduced
   D. the top man should state the expected conclusions

22. In attempting to motivate employees, rewards are considered preferable to punishment PRIMARILY because 22.____
   A. punishment seldom has any effect on human behavior
   B. punishment usually results in decreased production
   C. supervisors find it difficult to punish
   D. rewards are more likely to result in willing cooperation

23. In an attempt to combat the low morale in his organization, a high-level supervisor publicized an *open-door* policy to allow employees who wished to do so to come to him with their complaints. 23.____
Which of the following is LEAST likely to account for the fact that no employee came in with a complaint?
   A. Employees are generally reluctant to go over the heads of their immediate supervisors.
   B. The employees did not feel that management would help them.
   C. The low morale was not due to complaints association with the job
   D. The employees felt that they had more to lose than to gain.

24. It is MOST desirable to use written instructions rather than oral instructions for a particular job when 24.____
   A. a mistake on the job will not be serious
   B. the job can be completed in a short time
   C. there is no need to explain the job minutely
   D. the job involves many details

25. You have been asked to prepare for public distribution a statement dealing with a controversial matter. 25.____
Of the following approaches, the one which would usually be MOST effective is to present your department's point of view
   A. as tersely as possible with no reference to any other matters
   B. developed from ideas and facts well known to most readers
   C. and show all the statistical data and techniques which were used in arriving at it
   D. in such a way that the controversial parts are omitted

KEY (CORRECT ANSWERS)

1. D
2. D
3. C
4. C
5. A

6. D
7. A
8. B
9. A
10. C

11. C
12. C
13. D
14. B
15. A

16. A
17. C
18. B
19. D
20. C

21. B
22. D
23. C
24. D
25. B

TEST 3

DIRECTIONS: Each question or incomplete statement is followed by several suggested answers or completions. Select the one that BEST answers the question or completes the statement. *PRINT THE LETTER OF THE CORRECT ANSWER IN THE SPACE AT THE RIGHT.*

1. An administrator who supervises other supervisors makes it a practice to set deadline dates for completion of assignments. 1.____
   A NATURAL consequence of setting deadline dates is that
   A. supervisors will usually wait until the deadline date before they give projects their wholehearted attention
   B. projects are completed sooner than if no deadline dates are set
   C. such dates are ignored even though they are conspicuously posted
   D. the frequency of errors sharply increases resulting in an inability to meet deadlines

2. Assume that you are chairing a meeting of the members of your staff. You throw out a question to the group. No one answers your question immediately, so that you find yourself faced with silence. 2.____
   In the circumstances, it would probably be BEST for you to
   A. ask the member of the group who appears to be least attentive to repeat the question
   B. change the topic quickly
   C. repeat the question carefully, pronouncing each word, and if there is still no response, repeat the question an additional time
   D. wait for an answer since someone will usually say something to break the tension

3. Assume that you are holding a meeting with the members of your staff. John, a member of the unit, keeps sidetracking the subject of the discussion by bringing up extraneous matters. You deal with the situation by saying to him after he has raised an immaterial point, *"That's an interesting point John, but can you show me how it ties in with what we're talking about?"* 3.____
   Your approach in this situation would GENERALLY be considered
   A. *bad*; you have prevented the group from discussing not only extraneous matters but pertinent material as well
   B. *bad*; you have seriously humiliated John in front of the entire group
   C. *good*; you have pointed out how the discussion is straying from the main topic
   D. *good*; you have prevented John from presenting extraneous matters at future meetings

4. Assume that a senior supervisor is asked to supervise a group of staff personnel. The work of one of these staff men meets minimum standards of acceptability. However, this staff man constantly looks for something at which to take offense. In any conversation with either a fellow staff man or with a superior, he views the slightest criticism as a grave insult. 4.____

In this case, the senior supervisor should
A. advise the staff man that the next time he refuses to accept criticism, he will be severely reprimanded
B. ask member of the group for advice on how to deal with this staff man
C. make it a practice to speak calmly, slowly, and deliberately to this staff man and question him frequently to make sure that there is no breakdown in communications
D. recognize that professional help may be required and that this problem may not be conducive to a solution by a supervisor

5. Assume that you discover that one of the staff in preparing certain papers has made a serious mistake which has become obvious. 5.____
In dealing with this situation, it would be BEST for you to begin by
A. asking the employee how the mistake happened
B. asking the employee to read through the papers to see whether he can correct the mistake
C. pointing out to the employee that, while an occasional error is permissible, frequent errors can prove a source of embarrassment to all concerned
D. pointing to the mistake and asking the employee whether he realizes the consequences of the mistake

6. You desire to develop teamwork among the members of your staff. You are assigned a case which will require that two of the staff work together if the papers are to be prepared in time. You decided to assign two employees, whom you know to be close friends, to work on these papers. 6.____
Your action in this regard would GENERALLY be considered
A. *bad*; friends working together tend to do as little as they can get away with
B. *bad*; people who are friends socially often find that the bonds of friendship disintegrate in work situations
C. *good*; friends who are permitted to work together show their appreciation by utilizing every opportunity to reinforce the group leader's position of authority
D. *good*; the evidence suggests that more work can be done in this way

7. You notice that all of the employees, without exception, take lunch hours which in your view are excessively long. You call each of them to your desk and point out that unless this practice is brought to a stop, appropriate action will be taken. 7.____
The way in which you handled this problem would GENERALLY be considered
A. *proper*, primarily because a civil servant, no matter what his professional status, owes the public a full day's work for a full day's pay
B. *proper*, primarily because employees need to have a clear picture of the rewards and penalties that go with public employment
C. *improper*, primarily because group problems require group discussion which need not be formal in character
D. *improper*, primarily because professional personnel resent having such matters as lunch hours brought to their attention

8. In communicating with superiors or subordinates, it is well to bear in mind a phenomenon known as the *halo effect*. An example of this *halo effect* occurs when we 8.____
   A. employ informal language in a formal setting as a means of attracting attention
   B. ignore the advice of someone we distrust without evaluating the advice
   C. ask people to speak up who have a tendency to speak softly or occasionally indistinctly
   D. react to a piece of good work by inquiring into the motivations of those who did the work

9. Which of the following dangers is MOST likely to arise when a work group becomes too tightly knit? The 9.____
   A. group may appoint an informal leader who gradually sets policies and standards for the group to the detriment of the agency
   B. group may be reluctant to accept new employees as members
   C. quantity and quality of work produced may tend to diminish sharply despite the group's best efforts
   D. group may focus too strongly on employee benefits at inappropriate times

10. The overall managerial problem has become more complex because each group of management specialists will tend to view the interests of the enterprise in terms which are compatible with the survival or the increase of its special function. That is, each group will have a trained capacity for its own function and a *trained incapacity* to see its relation to the whole. 10.____
The *trained incapacity* to which the foregoing passage refers PROBABLY results from
   A. an imbalance in the number of specialists as compared with the number of generalists
   B. development by each specialized group of a certain dominant value or goal that shapes its entire way of doing things
   C. low morale accompanied by lackadaisical behavior by large segments of the managerial staff
   D. supervisory failure to inculcate pride in workmanship

11. Of the following, the MOST important responsibility of a supervisor in charge of a section is to 11.____
   A establish close personal relationships with each of his subordinates in the section
   B. insure that each subordinate in the section knows the full range of his duties and responsibilities
   C. maintain friendly relations with his immediate supervisor
   D. protect his subordinates from criticism from any source

12. The BEST way to get a good work output from employees is to 12.____
   A. hold over them the threat of disciplinary action or removal
   B. maintain a steady, unrelenting pressure on them
   C. show them that you can do anything they can do faster and better
   D win their respect and liking so they want to work for you

13. Supervisors should GENERALLY 13.____
    A. lean more toward management than toward their subordinates
    B. lean neither toward subordinates nor management
    C. lean more toward their subordinates than toward their management
    D. maintain a proper balance between management and subordinates

14. For a supervisor in charge of a section to ask occasionally the opinion of a subordinate concerning a problem is 14.____
    A. *desirable*; but it would be even better if the subordinate were consulted routinely on every problem
    B. *desirable*; subordinates may make good suggestions and will be pleased by being consulted
    C. *undesirable*; subordinates may be resentful if their advice is not followed
    D. *undesirable*; the supervisor should not attempt to shift his responsibilities to subordinates

15. The PRIMARY responsibility of a supervisor is to 15.____
    A. gain the confidence and make friends of all his subordinates
    B. get the work done properly
    C. satisfy his superior and gain his respect
    D. train the men in new methods for doing the work

16. In starting a work simplification study, the one of the following steps that should be taken FIRST is to 16.____
    A. break the work down into its elements
    B. draw up a chart of operations
    C. enlist the interest and cooperation of the personnel
    D. suggest alternative procedures

17. Of the following, the MOST important value of a manual of procedures is that it usually 17.____
    A. eliminates the need for on-the-job training
    B. decreases the span of control which can be exercised by individual supervisory personnel
    C. outlines methods of operation for ready reference
    D. provides concrete examples of work previously performed by employees

18. Reprimanding a subordinate when he has done something wrong should be done PRIMARILY in order to 18.____
    A. deter others from similar acts
    B. improve the subordinate in future performance
    C. maintain discipline
    D. uphold departmental rules

19. Most of the training of new employees in a public agency is USUALLY accomplished by 19.____
    A. formal classes
    B. general orientation
    C. internship
    D. on-the-job activities

20. You find that delivery of a certain item cannot possibly be made to a using agency by the date the using agency requested. 20.____
Of the following, the MOST advisable course of action for you to take FIRST is to
   A. cancel the order and inform the using agency
   B. discuss the problem with the using agency
   C. notify the using agency to obtain the item through direct purchase
   D. schedule the delivery for the earliest possible date

21. Assume that one of your subordinates has gotten into the habit of regularly and routinely referring every small problem which arises in his work to you. 21.____
In order to help him overcome this habit, it is generally MOST advisable for you to
   A. advise him that you do not have time to discuss each problem with him and that he should do whatever he wants
   B. ask your subordinate for his solution and approve any satisfactory approach that he suggests
   C. refuse to discuss such routine problems with him
   D. tell him that he should consider looking for another position if he does not feel competent to solve such routine problems

22. The BEST of the following reasons for developing understudies to supervisory staff is that this practice 22.____
   A. assures that capable staff will not leave their jobs since they are certain to be promoted
   B. helps to assure continued efficiency when persons in important positions leave their jobs
   C. improves morale by demonstrating to employees the opportunities for advancement
   D. provides an opportunity for giving on-the-job training

23. When a supervisor delegates some of his work to a subordinate, the 23.____
   A. supervisor retains final responsibility for the work
   B. supervisor should not check on the work until it has been completed
   C. subordinate assumes full responsibility for the successful completion of the work
   D. subordinate is likely to lose interest and get less satisfaction from the work

24. Sometimes it is necessary to give out written orders or to post written or typed information on a bulletin board rather than to merely give spoken orders. The supervisor must decide how he will do it. 24.____
In which of the following situations would it be BETTER for him to give written rather than spoken orders?
   A. He is going to reassign a man from one unit to another under his supervision.
   B. His staff must be informed of a permanent change in a complicated operating procedure.

C. A man must be transferred from a clerical unit to an operating unit.
D. He must order a group of staff men to do a difficult and tedious inventory job to which most of them are likely to object.

25. Of the following symbolic patterns, which one is NOT representative of a normal direction in which formal organizational communications flow? 25.____

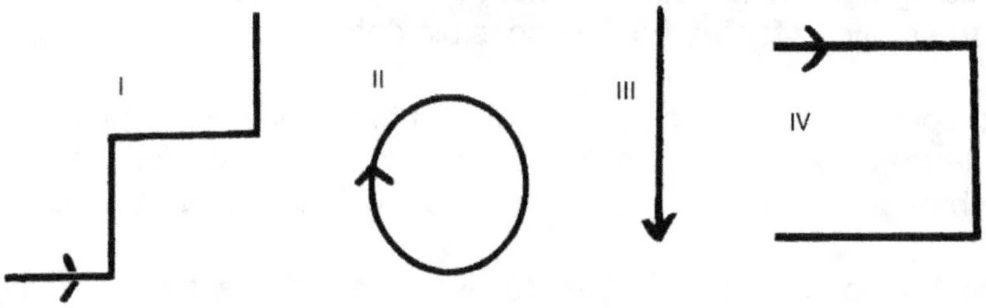

A. I B. II C. III D. IV

KEY (CORRECT ANSWERS)

1. B
2. D
3. C
4. D
5. A

6. D
7. C
8. B
9. B
10. B

11. B
12. D
13. D
14. B
15. B

16. C
17. C
18. B
19. D
20. B

21. B
22. B
23. A
24. B
25. B

EXAMINATION SECTION

TEST 1

DIRECTIONS: Each question or incomplete statement is followed by several suggested answers or completions. Select the one that BEST answers the question or completes the statement. *PRINT THE LETTER OF THE CORRECT ANSWER IN THE SPACE AT THE RIGHT.*

1. Which one of the following generalizations is MOST likely to be INACCURATE and lead to judgmental errors in communication? 1.____
   A. A supervisor must be able to read with understanding.
   B. Misunderstanding may lead to dislike.
   C. Anyone can listen to another person and understand what he means.
   D. It is usually desirable to let a speaker talk until he is finished.

2. Assume that, as a supervisor, you have been directed to inform your subordinates about the implementation of a new procedure which will affect their work. 2.____
   While communicating this information, you should do all of the following EXCEPT
   A. obtain the approval of your subordinates regarding the new procedure
   B. explain the reason for implementing the new procedure
   C. hold a staff meeting at a time convenient to most of your subordinates
   D. encourage a productive discussion of the new procedure

3. Assume that you are in charge of a section that handles requests for information on matters received from the public. One day, you observe that a clerk under your supervision is using a method to log-in requests for information that is different from the one specified by you in the past. Upon questioning the clerk, you discover that instructions changing the old procedure were delivered orally by your supervisor on a day on which you were absent from the office. 3.____
   Of the following, the MOST appropriate action for you to take is to
   A. tell the clerk to revert to the old procedure at once
   B. ask your supervisor for information about the change
   C. call your staff together and tell them that no existing procedure is to be changed unless you direct that it be done
   D. write a memo to your supervisor suggesting that all future changes in procedure are to be in writing and that they be directed to you

4. At the first meeting with your staff after appointment as a supervisor, you find considerable indifference and some hostility among the participants. 4.____
   Of the following, the MOST appropriate way to handle this situation is to
   A. disregard the attitudes displayed and continue to make your presentation until you have completed it
   B. discontinue your presentation but continue the meeting and attempt to find out the reasons for their attitudes

C. warm up your audience with some good-natured statements and anecdotes and then proceed with your presentation
D. discontinue the meeting and set up personal interviews with the staff members to try to find out the reason for their attitude

5. In order to start the training of a new employee, it has been a standard practice to have him read a manual of instructions or procedures. 5.____
This method is currently being replaced by the _____ method.
A. audio-visual
B. conference
C. lecture
D. programmed instruction

6. Of the following subjects, the one that can usually be successfully taught by a first-line supervisor who is training his subordinates is: 6.____
A. theory and philosophy of management
B. human relations
C. responsibilities of a supervisor
D. job skills

7. Assume that as supervisor you are training a clerk who is experiencing difficulty learning a new task. 7.____
Which of the following would be the LEAST effective approach to take when trying to solve this problem? To
A. ask questions which will reveal the clerk's understanding of the task
B. take a different approach in explaining the task
C. give the clerk an opportunity to ask questions about the task
D. make sure the clerk knows you are watching his work closely

8. One school of management and supervision involves participation by employees in the setting of group goals and in the sharing of responsibility for the operation of the unit. 8.____
If this philosophy were applied to a unit consisting of professional and clerical personnel, one should expect
A. the professional and clerical personnel to participate with equal effectiveness in operating areas and policy areas
B. the professional personnel to participate with greater effectiveness than the clerical personnel in policy areas
C. the clerical personnel to participate with greater effectiveness than the professional personnel in operating areas
D. greater participation by clerical personnel but with less responsibility for their actions

9. With regard to productivity, high morale among employees generally indicates a 9.____
A. history of high productivity
B. nearly absolute positive correlation with high productivity
C. predisposition to be productive under facilitating leadership and circumstances
D. complacency which has little effect on productivity

10. Assume that you are going to organize the professionals and clerks under your supervision into work groups or team of two or three employees. 10.____
Of the following, the step which is LEAST likely to foster the successful development of each group is to
   A. allow friends to work together in the group
   B. provide special help and attention to employees with no friends in their group
   C. frequently switch employees from group to group
   D. rotate jobs within the group in order to strengthen group identification

11. Following are four statements which might be made by an employee to his supervisor during a performance evaluation interview. 11.____
Which of the statements BEST provides a basis for developing a plan to improve the employee's performance?
   A. *I understand that you are dissatisfied with my work and I will try harder in the future.*
   B. *I feel that I've been making too many careless clerical errors recently.*
   C. *I am aware that I will be subject to disciplinary action if my work does not improve within one month.*
   D. *I understand that this interview is simply a requirement of your job and not a personal attack on me.*

12. Three months ago, Mr. Smith and his supervisor, Mrs. Jones, developed a plan which was intended to correct Mr. Smith's inadequate job performance. Now, during a follow-up interview, Mr. Smith, who thought his performance had satisfactorily improved, has been informed that Mrs. Jones is still dissatisfied with his work. 12.____
Of the following, it is MOST likely that the disagreement occurred because, when formulating the plan, they did NOT
   A. set realistic goals for Mr. Smith's performance
   B. set a reasonable time limit for Mr. Smith to effect his improvement in performance
   C. provide for adequate training to improve Mr. Smith's skills
   D. establish performance standards for measuring Mr. Smith's progress

13. When a supervisor delegates authority to subordinates, there are usually many problems to overcome, such as inadequately trained subordinates and poor planning. 13.____
All of the following are means of increasing the effectiveness of delegation EXCEPT:
   A. Defining assignments in the light of results expected
   B. Maintaining open lines of communication
   C. Establishing tight controls so that subordinates will stay within the bounds of the area of delegation
   D. Providing rewards for successful assumption of authority by a subordinate

14. Assume that one of your subordinates has arrived late for work several times during the current month. The last time he was late you had warned him that another unexcused lateness would result informal disciplinary action. If the employee arrives late for work again during this month, the FIRST action you should take is to 14.____
    A. give the employee a chance to explain this lateness
    B. give the employee a written copy of your warning
    C. tell the employee that you are recommending formal disciplinary action
    D. tell the employee that you will give him only one more chance before recommending formal disciplinary action

15. In trying to decide how many subordinates a manager can control directly, one of the determinants is how much the manager can reduce the frequency and time consumed in contacts with his subordinates. Of the following, the factor which LEAST influences the number and direction of these contacts is: 15.____
    A. How well the manager delegates authority
    B. The rate at which the organization is changing
    C. The control techniques used by the manager
    D. Whether the activity is line or staff

16. Systematic rotation of employees through lateral transfer within a government organization to provide for managerial development is 16.____
    A. *good*, because systematic rotation develops specialists who learn to do many jobs well
    B. *bad*, because the outsider upsets the status quo of the existing organization
    C. *good*, because rotation provides challenge and organizational flexibility
    D. *bad*, because it is upsetting to employees to be transferred within a service

17. Assume that you are required to provide an evaluation of the performance of your subordinates. Of the following factors, it is MOST important that the performance evaluation include a rating of each employee's 17.____
    A. initiative B. productivity C. intelligence D. personality

18. When preparing performance evaluations of your subordinates, one way to help assure that you are rating each employee fairly is to 18.____
    A. prepare a list of all employees and all the rating factors and rate all employees on one rating factor before going on to the next factor
    B. prepare a list of all your employees and all the rating factors and rate each employee on all factors before going on to the next employee
    C. discuss all the ratings you anticipate giving with another supervisor in order to obtain an unbiased opinion
    D. discuss each employee with his co-workers in order to obtain peer judgment of worth before doing any rating

19. A managerial plan which would include the GREATEST control is a plan which is 19.____
    A. spontaneous and geared to each new job that is received
    B. detailed and covering an extended time period
    C. long-range and generalized, allowing for various interpretations
    D. specific and prepared daily

20. Assume that you are preparing a report which includes statistical data covering increases in budget allocations of four agencies for the past ten years. 20.____
For you to represent the statistical data pictorially or graphically within the report is a
    A. *poor* idea, because you should be able to make statistical data understandable through the use of words
    B. *good* idea, because it is easier for the reader to understand pictorial representation rather than quantities of words conveying statistical data
    C. *poor* idea, because using pictorial representation in a report may make the report too expensive to print
    D. *good* idea, because a pictorial representation makes the report appear more attractive than the use of many words to convey the statistical data

---

KEY (CORRECT ANSWERS)

1.	C	11.	A
2.	A	12.	B
3.	B	13.	C
4.	D	14.	A
5.	D	15.	D
6.	D	16.	C
7.	D	17.	B
8.	B	18.	A
9.	C	19.	B
10.	C	20.	B

TEST 2

DIRECTIONS: Each question or incomplete statement is followed by several suggested answers or completions. Select the one that BEST answers the question or completes the statement. *PRINT THE LETTER OF THE CORRECT ANSWER IN THE SPACE AT THE RIGHT.*

1. Research studies have shown that supervisors of groups with high production records USUALLY 1.____
   A. give detailed instructions, constantly check on progress, and insist on approval of all decisions before implementation
   B. do considerable paperwork and other work similar to that performed by subordinates
   C. think of themselves as team members on the same level as others in the work group
   D. perform tasks traditionally associated with managerial functions

2. Mr. Smith, a bureau chief, is summoned by his agency's head in a conference to discuss Mr. Jones, an accountant who works in one of the divisions of his bureau. Mr. Jones has committed an error of such magnitude as to arouse the agency head's concern. 2.____
   After agreeing with the other conferees that a severe reprimand would be the appropriate punishment, Mr. Smith SHOULD
   A. arrange for Mr. Jones to explain the reasons for his error to the agency head
   B. send a memorandum to Mr. Jones, being careful that the language emphasizes the nature of the error rather than Mr. Jones' personal faults
   C. inform Mr. Jones' immediate supervisor of the conclusion reached at the conference, and let the supervisor take the necessary action
   D. suggest to the agency head that no additional action be taken against Mr. Jones because no further damage will be caused by the error

3. Assume that Ms. Thomson, a unit chief, has determined that the findings of an internal audit have been seriously distorted as a result of careless errors. The audit had been performed by a group of auditors in her unit and the errors were overlooked by the associate accountant in charge of the audit. Ms. Thomson has decided to delay discussing the matter with the associate accountant and the staff who performed the audit until she verifies certain details, which may require prolonged investigation. 3.____
   Mrs. Thomson's method of handling this situation is
   A. *appropriate*; employees should not be accused of wrongdoing until all the facts have been determined
   B. *inappropriate*; the employees involved may assume that the errors were considered unimportant
   C. *appropriate*; employees are more likely to change their behavior as a result of disciplinary action taken after a *cooling off* period
   D. *inappropriate*; the employees involved may have forgotten the details and become emotionally upset when confronted with the facts

4. After studying the financial situation in his agency, an administrative accountant decides to recommend centralization of certain accounting functions which are being performed in three different bureaus of the organization
The one of the following which is MOST likely to be a DISADVANTAE if this recommendation is implemented is that 4.____
   A. there may be less coordination of the accounting procedure because central direction is not so close to the day-to-day problems as the personnel handling them in each specialized accounting unit
   B. the higher management levels would not be able to make emergency decisions in as timely a manner as the more involved, lower-level administrators who are closer to the problem
   C. it is more difficult to focus the attention of the top management in order to resolve accounting problems because of the many other activities top management is involved in at the same time
   D. the accuracy of upward and inter-unit communication may be reduced because centralization may require insertion of more levels of administration in the chain of command

5. Of the following assumptions about the role of conflict in an organization, the one which is the MOST accurate statement of the approach of modern management theorists is that conflict 5.____
   A. can usually be avoided or controlled
   B. serves as a vital element in organizational change
   C. works against attainment of organizational goals
   D. provides a constructive outlet for problem employees

6. Which of the following is generally regarded as the BEST approach for a supervisor to follow in handling grievances brought by subordinates? 6.____
   A. Avoid becoming involved personally
   B. Involve the union representative in the first stage of discussion
   C. Settle the grievance as soon as possible
   D. Arrange for arbitration by a third party

7. Assume that supervisors of similar-sized accounting units in city, state, and federal offices were interviewed and observed at their work. It was found that the ways they acted in and viewed their roles tended to be very similar, regardless of who employed them.
Which of the following is the BEST explanation of this similarity 7.____
   A. A supervisor will ordinarily behave in conformance to his own self-image.
   B. Each role in an organization, including the supervisory role, calls for a distinct type of personality.
   C. The supervisor role reflects an exceptionally complex pattern of human response.
   D. The general nature of the duties and responsibilities of the supervisory position determines the role.

8. Which of the following is NOT consistent with the findings of recent research about the characteristics of successful top managers? 8.____
   A. They are *inner-directed* and not overly concerned with pleasing others.
   B. They are challenged by situations filled with high risk and ambiguity.
   C. They tend to stay on the same job for long periods of time.
   D. They consider it more important to handle critical assignments successfully than to do routine work well.

9. As a supervisor, you have to give subordinates operational guidelines. Of the following, the BEST reason for providing them with information about the overall objectives within which their operations fit is that the subordinates will 9.____
   A. be more likely to carry out the operation according to your expectations
   B. know that there is a legitimate reason for carrying out the operation in the way you have prescribed
   C. be more likely to handle unanticipated problems that may arise without having to take up your time
   D. more likely to transmit the operating instructions correctly to their subordinates

10. A supervisor holds frequent meetings with his staff. Of the following, the BEST approach he can take in order to elicit productive discussions at these meetings is for him to 10.____
   A. ask questions of those who attend
   B. include several levels of supervisors at the meetings
   C. hold the meetings at a specified time each week
   D. begin each meeting with a statement that discussion is welcomed

11. Of the following, the MOST important action that a supervisor can take to increase the productivity of a subordinate is to 11.____
   A. increase his uninterrupted work time
   B. increase the number of reproducing machines available in the office
   C. provide clerical assistance whenever he requests it
   D. reduce the number of his assigned tasks

12. Assume that, as a supervisor, you find out that you often must countermand or modify your original staff memos. If this practice continues, which one of the following situations is MOST likely to occur? The 12.____
   A. staff will not bother to read your memos
   B. office files will become cluttered
   C. staff will delay acting on your memos
   D. memos will be treated routinely

13. In making management decisions, the committee approach is often used by managers. Of the following, the BEST reason for using this approach is to 13.____
   A. prevent any one individual from assuming too much authority
   B. allow the manager to bring a wider range of experience and judgment to bear on the problem

C. allow the participation of all staff members, which will make them feel more committed to the decisions reached
D. permit the rapid transmission of information about decisions reached to the staff members concerned

14. In establishing standards for the measurement of the performance of a management project team, it is MOST important for the project manager to 14.____
A. identify and define the objectives of the project
B. determine the number of people who will be assigned to the project team
C. evaluate the skills of the staff who will be assigned to the project team
D. estimate fairly accurately the length of time required to complete each phase of the project

15. It is virtually impossible to tell an employee either that he is not good as another employee or that he does not measure up to a desirable level of performance, without having him feel threatened, rejected, and discouraged. 15.____
In accordance with the foregoing observation, a supervisor who is concerned about the performance of the less efficient members of his staff should realize that
A. he might obtain better results by not discussing the quality and quantity of their work with them, but by relying instead on the written evaluation of their performance to motivate their improvement
B. since he is required to discuss their performance with them, he should do so in words of encouragement and in so friendly a manner as to not destroy their morale
C. he might discuss their work in a general way, without mentioning any of the specifics about the quality of their performance, with the expectation that they would understand the full implications of his talk
D. he should make it a point, while telling them of their poor performance, to mention that their work is as good as that of some of the other employees in the unit

16. Some advocates of management-by-objectives procedures in public agencies have been urging that this method of operations be expanded to encompass all agencies of the government, for one or more of the following reasons, not all of which may be correct: 16.____
I. The MBO method is likely to succeed because it embraces the practice of setting near-term goals for the subordinate manager, reviewing accomplishments at an appropriate time, and repeating this process indefinitely
II. Provision for authority to perform the tasks assigned as goals in the MBO method is normally not needed because targets are set in quantitative or qualitative terms and specific times for accomplishment are arranged in short-term, repetitive intervals
III. Many other appraisal-of-performance programs failed because both supervisors and subordinates resisted them, while the MBO approach is not instituted until there is an organizational commitment to it
IV. Personal accountability is clearly established through the MBO approach because verifiable results are set up in the process of formulating the targets

Which of the choices below includes ALL of the foregoing statements that are CORRECT?

A. I, III B. II, IV C. I, II, III, IV D. I, III, IV

17. In preparing an organizational structure, the PRINCIPAL guideline for locating staff units is to place them 17.____
    A. all under a common supervisor
    B. as close as possible to the activities they serve
    C. as close to the chief executive as possible without over-extending his span of control
    D. at the lowest operational level

18. The relative importance of any unit in a department can be LEAST reliably judged by the 18.____
    A. amount of office space allocated to the unit
    B. number of employees in the unit
    C. rank of the individual who heads the unit
    D. rank of the individual to whom the unit head reports directly

19. Those who favor Planning-Programming-Budgeting Systems (PPBS) as a new method of governmental financial administration emphasize that PPBS 19.____
    A. applies statistical measurements which correlate highly with criteria
    B. makes possible economic systems analysis, including an explicit examination of alternatives
    C. makes available scarce government resources which can be coordinated on a government-wide basis and shared between local units of government
    D. shifts the emphasis in budgeting methods to an automated system of data processing

20. The term applied to computer processing which processes data concurrently with a given activity and provides results soon enough to influence the selection of a course of action is _____ processing. 20.____
    A. realtime B. batch
    C. random access D. integrated data

KEY (CORRECT ANSWERS)

1.	D	11.	A
2.	C	12.	C
3.	B	13.	B
4.	D	14.	A
5.	B	15.	B
6.	C	16.	D
7.	D	17.	B
8.	C	18.	B
9.	C	19.	B
10.	A	20.	A

READING COMPREHENSION
UNDERSTANDING AND INTERPRETING WRITTEN MATERIAL

EXAMINATION SECTION

TEST 1

DIRECTIONS: Each question or incomplete statement is followed by several suggested answers or completions. Select the one that BEST answers the question or completes the statement. *PRINT THE LETTER OF THE CORRECT ANSWER IN THE SPACE AT THE RIGHT.*

Questions 1-3.

DIRECTIONS: Questions 1 through 3 are to be answered SOLELY on the basis of the following passage.

Every organization needs a systematic method of checking its operations as a means to increase efficiency and promote economy. Many successful private firms have instituted a system of audit or internal inspections to accomplish these ends. Law enforcement organizations, which have an extremely important service to *sell*, should be no less zealous in developing efficiency and economy in their operations. Periodic, organized, and systematic inspections are one means of promoting the achievement of these objectives. The necessity of an organized inspection system is perhaps greatest in those law enforcement groups which have grown to such a size that the principal officer can no longer personally supervise or be cognizant of every action taken. Smooth and effective operation demands that the head of the organization have at hand some tool with which he can study and enforce general policies and procedure and also direct compliance with day-to-day orders, most of which are put into execution outside his sight and hearing. A good inspection system can serve as that tool.

1. The central thought of the above passage is that a system of inspections within a police department 1.____
   A. is unnecessary for a department in which the principal officer can personally supervise all official actions taken
   B. should be instituted at the first indication that there is any deterioration in job performance by the force
   C. should be decentralized and administered by first-line supervisory officers
   D. is an important aid to the police administrator in the accomplishment of law enforcement objectives

2. The MOST accurate of the following statements concerning the need for an organized inspection system in a law enforcement organization is: It is 2.____
   A. never needed in an organization of small size where the principal officer can give personal supervision
   B. most needed where the size of the organization prevents direct supervision by the principal officer
   C. more needed in law enforcement organizations than in private firms
   D. especially needed in an organization about to embark upon a needed expansion of services

3. According to the above passage, the head of the police organization utilizes the internal inspection system 3.____
   A. as a tool which must be constantly re-examined in the light of changing demands for police service
   B. as an administrative technique to increase efficiency and promote economy
   C. by personally visiting those areas of police operation which are outside his sight and hearing
   D. to augment the control of local commanders over detailed field operations

Questions 4-10.

DIRECTIONS: Questions 4 through 10 are to be answered SOLELY on the basis of the following passage.

Job evaluation and job rating systems are intended to introduce scientific procedures. Any type of approach, when properly used, will give satisfactory results. The Point System, when properly validated by actual use, is more likely to be suitable for general use than the ranking system. In many aspects, the Factor Comparison Plan is a point system tied to money values. Of course, there may be another system that combines the ranking system with the point system, especially during the initial stages of the development of the program. After the program has been in use for some time, the tendency is to drop off the ranking phase and continue the use of the point system.

In the ranking system of rating of jobs, every job within the plant is arranged in some order, either from the one with the simplest qualifications to the one with maximum requirements, or in the reverse order. This system should be preceded by careful job analysis and the writing of accurate job descriptions before the rating process is undertaken. It is possible, of course, to take the jobs as they are found in the business enterprise and use the names as they are without any attempt at standardization, and merely rank them according to the general overall impression of the raters. Such a procedure is certain to fall short of what may reasonably be expected of job rating. Another procedure that is in reality merely a modification of the simple rating described above is to establish a series of grades or zones and arrange all he jobs in the plant into groups within these grades and zones. The practice in most common use is to arrange all the jobs in the plant according to their requirements by rating them and then to establish the classification or groups.

The actual ranking of jobs may be done by one individual, several individuals, or a committee. If several individuals are working independently on the task, it will usually be found that, in general, they agree but that their rankings vary in certain details. A conference between the individuals, with each person giving his reasons why he rated one way or another, usually produces agreement. The detailed job descriptions are particularly helpful when there is disagreement among raters as to the rating of certain jobs. It is not only possible but desirable to have workers participate in the construction of the job description and in rating the job.

4. The MAIN theme of this passage is 4.____
   A. the elimination of bias in job rating
   B. the rating of jobs by the ranking system
   C. the need or accuracy in allocating points in the point system
   D. pitfalls to avoid in selecting key jobs in the Factor Comparison Plan

5. The ranking system of rating jobs consists MAINLY of 5.____
   A. attaching a point value to each ratable factor of each job prior to establishing an equitable pay scale
   B. arranging every job in the organization in descending order and then following this up with a job analysis of the key jobs
   C. preparing accurate job descriptions after a job analysis and then arranging all jobs either in ascending or descending order based on job requirements
   D. arbitrarily establishing a hierarchy of job classes and grades and then fitting each job into a specific class and grade based on the opinions of unit supervisors

6. The above passage states that the system of classifying jobs MOST used in an organization is to 6.____
   A. organize all jobs in the organization in accordance with their requirements and then create categories or clusters of jobs
   B. classify all jobs in the organization according to the titles and rank by which they are currently known in the organization
   C. establish a pre-arranged series of grades or zones and then fit all jobs into one of the grades or zones
   D. determine the salary currently being paid for each job and then rank the jobs in order according to salary

7. According to the above passage, experience has shown that when a group of raters is assigned to the job evaluation task and each individual rates independently of the others, the raters GENERALLY 7.____
   A. *agree* with respect to all aspects of their rankings
   B. *disagree* with respect to all or nearly all aspects of the rankings
   C. *disagree* on overall ratings, but agree on specific rating factors
   D. *agree* on overall rankings, but have some variance in some details

8. The above passage states that the use of a detailed job description is of special value when 8.____
   A. employees of an organization have participated in the preliminary step involved in actual preparation of the job description
   B. labor representatives are not participating in ranking of the jobs
   C. an individual rater who is unsure of himself is ranking the jobs
   D. a group of raters is having difficulty reaching unanimity with respect to ranking a certain job

9. A comparison of the various rating systems as described in the above passage shows that 9.____
   A. the ranking system is not as appropriate for general use as a properly validated point system
   B. the point system is the same as the Factor Comparison Plan except that it places greater emphasis on money

C. no system is capable of combining the point system and the Factor Comparison Plan
D. the point system will be discontinued last when used in combination with the Factor comparison System

10. The above passage implies that the PRINCIPAL reason for creating job evaluation and rating systems was to help 10.____
A. overcome union opposition to existing salary plans
B. base wage determination on a more objective and orderly foundation
C. eliminate personal bias on the part of the trained scientific job evaluators
D. management determine if it was overpricing the various jobs in the organizational hierarchy

Questions 11-13.

DIRECTIONS: Questions 11 through 13 are to be answered SOLELY on the basis of the following passage.

The common sense character of the merit system seems so natural to most Americans that many people wonder why it should ever have been inoperative. After all, the American economic system, the most phenomenal the world has ever known, is also founded on a rugged selective process which emphasizes the personal qualities of capacity, industriousness, and productivity. The criteria may not have always been appropriate and competition has not always been fair, but competition there was, and the responsibilities and the rewards—with exceptions, of course—have gone to those who could measure up in terms of intelligence, knowledge, or perseverance. This has been true not only in the economic area, in the money-making process, but also in achievement in the professions and other walks of life.

11. According to the above passage, economic rewards in the United State have 11.____
A. always been based on appropriate, fair criteria
B. only recently been based on a competitive system
C. not going to people who compete too ruggedly
D. usually gone to those people with intelligence, knowledge, and perseverance

12. According to the above passage, a merit system is 12.____
A. an unfair criterion on which to base rewards
B. unnatural to anyone who is not American
C. based only on common sense
D. based on the same principles as the American economic system

13. According to the above passage, it is MOST accurate to say that 13.____
A. the United States has always had a civil service merit system
B. civil service employees are very rugged
C. the American economic system has always been based on a merit objective
D. competition is unique to the American way of life

Questions 14-15.

DIRECTIONS: Questions 14 and 15 are to be answered SOLELY on the basis of the following passage.

In-basket tests are often used to assess managerial potential. The exercise consists of a set of papers that would be likely to be found in the in-basket of an administrator or manager at any given time, and requires the individuals participating in the examination to indicate how they would dispose of each item found in the in-basket. In order to handle the in-basket effectively, they must successfully manage their time, refer and assign some work to subordinates, juggle potentially conflicting appointments and meetings, and arrange for follow-up of problems generated by the items in the in-basket. In other words, the in-basket test is attempting to evaluate the participants' abilities to organize their work, set priorities, delegate, control, and make decisions.

14. According to the above passage, to succeed in an in-basket test, an administrator must 14.____
    A. be able to read very quickly
    B. have a great deal of technical knowledge
    C. know when to delegate work
    D. arrange a lot of appointments and meetings

15. According to the above passage, all of the following abilities are indications of managerial potential EXCEPT the ability to 15.____
    A. organize and control
    B. manage time
    C. write effective reports
    D. make appropriate decisions

Questions 16-19.

DIRECTIONS: Questions 16 through 19 are to be answered SOLELY on the basis of the following passage.

A personnel researcher has at his disposal various approaches for obtaining information, analyzing it, and arriving at conclusions that have value in predicting and affecting the behavior of people at work. The type of method to be used depends on such factors as the nature of the research problem, the available data, and the attitudes of those people being studied to the various kinds of approaches. While the experimental approach, with its use of control groups, is the most refined type of study, there are others that are often found useful in personnel research. Surveys, in which the researcher obtains facts on a problem from a variety of sources, are employed in research on wages, fringe benefits, and labor relations. Historical studies are used to trace the development of problems in order to understand them better and to isolate possible causative factors. Case studies are generally developed to explore all the details of a particular problem that is representative of other similar problems. A researcher chooses the most appropriate form of study for the problem he is investigating. He should recognize, however, that the experimental method, commonly referred to as the scientific method, if used validly and reliably, gives the most conclusive results.

16. The above passage discusses several approaches used to obtain information on particular problems. 16.____
Which of the following may be MOST reasonably concluded from the passage?
A(n)
   A. historical study cannot determine causative factors
   B. survey is often used in research on fringe benefits
   C. case study is usually used to explore a problem that is unique and unrelated to other problems
   D. experimental study is used when the scientific approach to a problem fails

17. According to the above passage, all of the following are factors that may determine the type of approach a researcher uses EXCEPT 17.____
   A. the attitudes of people toward being used in control groups
   B. the number of available sources
   C. his desire to isolate possible causative factors
   D. the degree of accuracy he requires

18. The words *scientific method*, as used in the last sentence of the above passage, refer to a type of study which, according to the above passage 18.____
   A. uses a variety of sources
   B. traces the development of problems
   C. uses control groups
   D. analyzes the details of a representative problem

19. Which of the following can be MOST reasonably concluded from the above passage? 19.____
In obtaining and analyzing information on a particular problem, a researcher employs the method which is the
   A. most accurate
   B. most suitable
   C. least expensive
   D. least time-consuming

Questions 20-25.

DIRECTIONS: Questions 20 through 25 are to be answered SOLELY on the basis of the following passage.

The quality of the voice of a worker is an important factor in conveying to clients and co-workers his attitude and, to some degree, his character. The human voice, when not consciously disguised, may reflect a person's mood, temper, and personality. It has been shown in several experiments that certain character traits can be assessed with better than chance accuracy through listening to the voice of an unknown person who cannot be seen.

Since one of the objectives of the worker is to put clients at ease and to present an encouraging and comfortable atmosphere, a harsh, shrill, or loud voice could have a negative effect. A client who displays emotions of anger or resentment would probably be provoked even further by a caustic tone. In a face-to-face situation, an unpleasant voice may be compensated for, to some degree, by a concerned and kind facial expression. However, when one speaks on the telephone, the expression on one's face cannot be seen by the listener. A supervising clerk who wishes to represent himself effectively to clients should try to eliminate as many faults as possible in striving to develop desirable voice qualities.

20. If a worker uses a sarcastic tone while interviewing a resentful client, the client, according to the above passage, would MOST likely 20.____
    A. avoid the face-to-face problem
    B. be ashamed of his behavior
    C. become more resentful
    D. be provoked to violence

21. According to the passage, experiments comparing voice and character traits have demonstrated that 21.____
    A. prospects for improving an unpleasant voice through training are better than chance
    B. the voice can be altered to project many different psychological characteristics
    C. the quality of the human voice reveals more about the speaker than his words do
    D. the speaker's voice tells the hearer something about the speaker's personality

22. Which of the following, according to the above passage, is a person's voice MOST likely to reveal? 22.____
    His
    A. prejudices
    B. intelligence
    C. social awareness
    D. temperament

23. It may be MOST reasonably concluded from the above passage that an interested and sympathetic expression on the face of a worker 23.____
    A. may induce a client to feel certain he will receive welfare benefits
    B. will eliminate the need for pleasant vocal qualities in the interviewer
    C. may help to make up for an unpleasant voice in the interviewer
    D. is desirable as the interviewer speaks on the telephone to a client

24. Of the following, the MOST reasonable implication of the above paragraph is that a worker should, when speaking to a client, control and use his voice to 24.____
    A. simulate a feeling of interest in the problems of the client
    B. express his emotions directly and adequately
    C. help produce in the client a sense of comfort and security
    D. reflect his own true personality

25. It may be concluded from the above passage that the PARTICULAR reason for a worker to pay special attention to modulating her voice when talking on the phone to a client is that, during a telephone conversation 25.____
    A. there is a necessity to compensate for the way in which a telephone distorts the voice
    B. the voice of the worker is a reflection of her mood and character
    C. the client can react only on the basis of the voice and words she hears
    D. the client may have difficulty getting a clear understanding over the telephone

KEY (CORRECT ANSWERS)

1.	D	11.	D
2.	B	12.	D
3.	B	13.	C
4.	B	14.	C
5.	C	15.	C
6.	A	16.	B
7.	D	17.	D
8.	D	18.	C
9.	A	19.	B
10.	B	20.	C

21.	D
22.	D
23.	C
24.	C
25.	C

TEST 2

DIRECTIONS: Each question or incomplete statement is followed by several suggested answers or completions. Select the one that BEST answers the question or completes the statement. *PRINT THE LETTER OF THE CORRECT ANSWER IN THE SPACE AT THE RIGHT.*

Questions 1-3.

DIRECTIONS: Questions 1 through 3 are to be answered SOLELY on the basis of the following paragraph.

Suppose you are given the job of printing, collating, and stapling 8,000 copies of a ten-page booklet as soon as possible. You have available one photo-offset machine, a collator with an automatic stapler, and the personnel to operate these machines. All will be available for however long the job takes to complete. The photo-offset machine prints 5,000 impressions an hour, and it takes about 15 minutes to set up a plate. The collator, including time for insertion of pages and stapling, can process about 2,000 booklets an hour. (Answers should be based on the assumption that there are no breakdowns or delays.)

1. Assuming that all the printing is finished before the collating is started, if the job is given to you late Monday and your section can begin work the next day and is able to devote seven hours a day, Monday through Friday, to the job until it is finished, what is the BEST estimate of when the job will be finished? 1.____
   A. Wednesday afternoon of the same week
   B. Thursday morning of the same week
   C. Friday morning of the same week
   D. Monday morning of the next week

2. An operator suggests to you that instead of completing all the printing and then beginning collating and stapling, you first print all the pages for 4,000 booklets, so that they can be collated and stapled while the last 4,000 pages are being printed. 2.____
   If you accepted this suggestion, the job would be completed
   A. sooner but would require more man-hours
   B at the same time using either method
   C. later and would require more man-hours
   D. sooner but there would be more wear and tear on the plates

3. Assume that you have the same assignment and equipment as described above, but 16,000 copies of the booklet are needed instead of 8,000. 3.____
   If you decided to print 8,000 complete booklets, then collate and staple them while you started printing the next 8,000 booklets, which of the following statements would MOST accurately describe the relationship between this new method and your original method of printing all the booklets at one time, and then collating and stapling them? The
   A. job would be completed at the same time regardless of the method used
   B. new method would result in the job's being completed 3½ hours earlier
   C. original method would result in the job's being completed an hour later
   D. new method would result in the job's being completed 1½ hours earlier

Questions 4-6.

DIRECTIONS: Questions 4 through 6 are to be answered SOLELY on the basis of the following passage.

When using words like company, association, council, committee, and board in place of the full official name, the writer should not capitalize these short forms unless he intends them to invoke the full force of the institution's authority. In legal contracts, in minutes, or in formal correspondence where one is speaking formally and officially on behalf of the company, the term Company is usually capitalized, but in ordinary usage, where it is not essential to load the short form with this significance, capitalization would be excessive. (Example: The company will have many good openings for graduates this June.)

The treatment recommended for short forms of place names is essentially the same as that recommended for short forms of organizational names. In general, we capitalize the full form but not the short form. If Park Avenue is referred to in one sentence, then the *avenue* is sufficient in subsequent references. The same is true with words like building, hotel, station, and airport, which are capitalized when part of a proper name changed (Pan Am Building, Hotel Plaza, Union Station, O'Hare Airport), but are simply lower-cased when replacing these specific names.

4. The above passage states that USUALLY the short forms of names of organizations — 4.____
   - A. and places should not be capitalized
   - B. and places should be capitalized
   - C. should not be capitalized, but the short forms of names of places should be capitalized
   - D. should be capitalized, but the short forms of names of places should not be capitalized

5. The above passage states that in legal contracts, in minutes, and in formal correspondence, the short forms of names of organizations should — 5.____
   - A. usually not be capitalized
   - B. usually be capitalized
   - C. usually not be used
   - D. never be used

6. It can be inferred from the above passage that decisions regarding when to capitalize certain words — 6.____
   - A. should be left to the discretion of the writer
   - B. should be based on generally accepted rules
   - C. depend on the total number of words capitalized
   - D. are of minor importance

Questions 7-10.

DIRECTIONS: Questions 7 through 10 are to be answered SOLELY on the basis of the following passage.

Use of the systems and procedures approach to office management is revolutionizing the supervision of office work. This approach views an enterprise as an entity which seeks to fulfill definite objectives. Systems and procedures help to organize repetitive work into a routine, thus reducing the amount of decision making required for its accomplishment. As a result, employees are guided in their efforts and perform only necessary work. Supervisors are relieved of any details of execution and are free to attend to more important work. Establishing work guides which require that identical tasks be performed the same way each time permits standardization of forms, machine operations, work methods, and controls. This approach also reduces the probability of errors. Any error committed is usually discovered quickly because the incorrect work does not meet the requirement of the work guides. Errors are also reduced through work specialization, which allows each employee to become thoroughly proficient in a particular type of work. Such proficiency also tends to improve the morale of the employees.

7. The above passage states that the accuracy of an employee's work is INCREASED by 7.____
   A. using the work specialization approach
   B. employing a probability sample
   C. requiring him to shift at one time into different types of tasks
   D. having his supervisor check each detail of work execution

8. Of the following, which one BEST expresses the main theme of the above passage? The 8.____
   A. advantages and disadvantages of the systems and procedures approach to office management
   B. effectiveness of the systems and procedures approach to office management in developing skills
   C. systems and procedures approach to office management as it relates to office costs
   D. advantages of the systems and procedures approach to office management for supervisors and office workers

9. Work guides are LEAST likely to be used when 9.____
   A. standardized forms are used
   B. a particular office task is distinct and different from all others
   C. identical tasks are to be performed in identical ways
   D. similar work methods are expected from each employee

10. According to the above passage, when an employee makes a work error, it USUALLY 10.____
   A. is quickly corrected by the supervisor
   B. necessitates a change in the work guides
   C. can be detected quickly if work guides are in use
   D. increases the probability of further errors by that employee

Questions 11-12.

DIRECTIONS: Questions 11 and 12 are to be answered SOLELY on the basis of the following passage.

The coordination of the many activities of a large public agency is absolutely essential. Coordination, as an administrative principle, must be distinguished from and is independent of cooperation. Coordination can be of either the horizontal or the vertical type. In large organizations, the objectives of vertical coordination are achieved by the transmission of orders and statements of policy down through the various levels of authority. It is an accepted generalization that the more authoritarian the organization, the more easily may vertical coordination be accomplished. Horizontal coordination is arrived through staff work, administrative management, and conferences of administrators of equal rank. It is obvious that of the two types of coordination, the vertical kind is more important, for at best horizontal coordination only supplements the coordination effected up and down the line,

11. According to the above passage, the ease with which vertical coordination is achieved in a large agency depends upon 11.____
    A. the extent to which control is firmly exercised from above
    B. the objectives that have been established for the agency
    C. the importance attached by employees to the orders and statements of policy transmitted through the agency
    D. the cooperation obtained at the various levels of authority

12. According to the above passage, 12.____
    A. vertical coordination is dependent for its success upon horizontal coordination
    B. one type of coordination may work in opposition to the other
    C. similar methods may be used to achieve both types of coordination
    D. horizontal coordination is at most an addition to vertical coordination

Questions 13-17.

DIRECTIONS: Questions 13 through 17 are to be answered SOLELY on the basis of the following situation.

Assume that you are a newly appointed supervisor in the same unit in which you have been acting as a provisional for some time. You have in your unit the following workers:

WORKER I: He has always been an efficient worker. In a number of his cases, the clients have recently begun to complain that they cannot manage on the departmental budget.

WORKER II: He has been under selective supervision for some time as an experienced, competent worker. He now begins to be late for his supervisory conferences and to stress how much work he has to do.

WORKER III: He has been making considerable improvement in his ability to handle the details of his job. He now tells you, during an individual conference, that he does not need such close supervision and that he wants to operate more independently. He says that Worker II is always available when he needs a little information or help but, in general, he can manage very well by himself.

WORKER IV: He brings you a complex case for decision as to eligibility. Discussion of the case brings out the fact that he has failed to consider all the available resources adequately but has stressed the family's needs to include every extra item in the budget. This is the third case of a similar nature that his worker has brought to you recently. This worker and Worker I work in adjacent territory and are rather friendly.

In the following questions, select the option that describes the method of dealing with these workers that illustrate BEST supervisory practice.

13. With respect to supervision of Worker I, the assistant supervisor should 13.____
   A. discuss with the worker, in an individual conference, any problems that he may be having due to the increase in the cost of living
   B. plan a group conference for the unit around budgeting, as both Workers I and IV seem to be having budgetary difficulties
   C. discuss with Workers I and IV together the meaning of money as acceptance or rejection to the clients
   D. discuss with Worker I the budgetary data in each case in relation to each client's situation

14. With respect to supervision of Worker II, the supervisory should 14.____
   A. move slowly with this worker and give him time to learn that the supervisor's official appointment has not changed his attitudes or methods of supervision
   B. discuss the worker's change of attitude and asks him to analyze the reasons for his change in behavior
   C. take time to show the worker how he is avoiding his responsibility in the supervisor-worker relationship and that he is resisting supervision
   D. hold an evaluatory conference with the worker and show him how he is taking over responsibilities that are not his by providing supervision for Worker III

15. With respect to supervision of Worker III, the supervisor should discuss with this worker 15.____
   A. why he would rather have supervision from Worker II than from the supervisor
   B. the necessity for further improvement before he can go on selective supervision
   C. an analysis of the improvement that has been made and the extent to which the worker is able to handle the total job for which he is responsible
   D. the responsibility of the supervisor to see that clients receive adequate service

16. With respect to supervision of Worker IV, the supervisor should 16.____
   A. show the worker that resources figures are incomplete but that even if they were complete, the family would probably be eligible for assistance
   B. ask the worker why he is so protective of these families since there are three cases so similar

C. discuss with the worker all three cases at the same time so that the worker may see his own role in the three situations
D. discuss with the worker the reasons for departmental policies and procedures around budgeting

17. With respect to supervision of Workers I and IV, since these two workers are friends and would seem to be influencing each other, the supervisor should 17.____
A. hold a joint conference with them both, pointing out how they should clear with the supervisor and not make their own rules together
B. handle the problems of each separately in individual conferences
C. separate them by transferring one to another territory or another unit
D. take up the problem of workers asking help of each other rather than from the supervisor in a group meeting

Questions 18-20.

DIRECTIONS: Questions 18 through 20 are to be answered SOLELY on the basis of the following passage.

One of the key supervisory problems in a large municipal recreation department is that many leaders are assigned to isolated playgrounds or small centers, where it is difficult to observe their work regularly. Often their facilities are extremely limited. In such settings, as well as in larger recreation centers, where many recreation leaders tend to have other jobs as well, there tends to be a low level of morale and incentive. Still, it is the supervisor's task to help recreation personnel to develop pride in their work and to maintain a high level of performance. With isolated leaders, the supervisor may give advice or assistance. Leaders may be assigned to different tasks or settings during the year to maximize their productivity and provide new challenges. When it is clear that leaders are no willing to make a real effort to contribute to the department, the possibility of penalties must be considered, within the scope of departmental policy and the union contract. However, the supervisor should be constructive, encourage and assist workers to take a greater interest in their work, be innovative, and try to raise morale and to improve performance in positive ways.

18. The one of the following that would the MOST appropriate title for the above passage is 18.____
A. Small Community Centers – Pro and Con
B. Planning Better Recreation Programs
C. The Supervisor's Task in Upgrading Personnel Performance
D. The Supervisor and the Municipal Union – Rights and Obligations

19. The above passage makes clear that recreation leadership performance in all recreation playgrounds and centers throughout a large city is 19.____
A. generally above average, with good morale on the part of most recreation leaders
B. beyond description since no one has ever observed or evaluated recreation leaders

C. a key test of the personnel department's effort to develop more effective hiring standards
D. of mixed quality, with many recreation leaders having poor morale and a low level of achievement

20. According to the above passage, the supervisor's role is to 20.____
A. use disciplinary action as his major tool in upgrading performance
B. tolerate the lack of effort of individual employees since they are assigned to isolated playgrounds or small centers
C. employ encouragement, advice, and, when appropriate, disciplinary action to improve performance
D. inform the county supervisor whenever malfeasance or idleness is detected

Questions 21-25.

DIRECTIONS: Questions 21 through 25 are to be answered SOLELY on the basis of the following passage.

EMPLOYEE LEAVE REGULATIONS

Peter Smith, as a full-time permanent city employee under the Career and Salary Plan, earns an *annual leave allowance*. This consists of a certain number of days off a year with pay and may be used for vacation, personal business, and for observing religious holidays. As a newly appointed employee, during his first 8 years of city service, he will earn an annual leave allowance of 20 days off a year (an average of $1^2/_3$ days off a month). After he has finished 8 full years of working for the city, he will begin earning an additional 5 days off a year. His annual leave allowance, therefore, will then be 25 days a year and will remain at this amount for seven full years. He will begin earning an additional two days off a year at this amount for seven full years. He will begin earning an additional two days off a year after he has completed a total of 15 years of city employment. Therefore, in his sixteenth year of working for the city, Mr. Smith will be earning 27 days off a year as his annual leave allowance (an average of 2¼ days off a month).

A *sick leave allowance* of one day a month is also given to Mr. Smith, but it can be used only in cases of actual illness. When Mr. Smith returns to work after using sick leave allowance, he must have a doctor's note if the absence is for a total of more than 3 days, but he may also be required to show a doctor's note for absences of 1, 2, or 3 days.

21. According to the above passage, Mr. Smith's annual leave allowance consists of a certain number of days off a year which he 21.____
A. does not get paid for
B. gets paid for at time and a half
C. may use for personal business
D. may not use for observing religious holidays

22. According to the above passage, after Mr. Smith has been working for the city for 9 years, his annual leave allowance will be _____ days a year. 22.____
A. 20 B. 25 C. 27 D. 37

23. According to the above passage, Mr. Smith will begin earning an average of 2 days off a month as his annual leave allowance after he has worked for the city for _____ full years. 23.____
    A. 7 B. 8 C. 15 D. 17

24. According to the above passage, Mr. Smith is given a sick leave allowance of 24.____
    A. 1 day every 2 months
    B. 1 day per month
    C. $1^{2}/_{3}$ days per month
    D. $2\frac{1}{4}$ days a month

25. According to the above passage, when he uses sick leave allowance, Mr. Smith may be required to show a doctor's note 25.____
    A. even if his absence is for only 1 day
    B. only if his absence is for more than 2 days
    C. only if his absence is for more than 3 days
    D. only if his absence is for 3 days or more

KEY (CORRECT ANSWERS)

1. C
2. C
3. D
4. A
5. B
6. B
7. A
8. D
9. B
10. C
11. A
12. D
13. D
14. A
15. C
16. C
17. B
18. C
19. D
20. C
21. C
22. B
23. C
24. B
25. A

TEST 3

DIRECTIONS: Each question or incomplete statement is followed by several suggested answers or completions. Select the one that BEST answers the question or completes the statement. *PRINT THE LETTER OF THE CORRECT ANSWER IN THE SPACE AT THE RIGHT.*

Questions 1-6.

DIRECTIONS: Questions 1 through 6 are to be answered SOLELY on the basis of the following passage.

A folder is made of a sheet of heavy paper (manila, kraft, pressboard, or red rope stock) that has been folded once so that the back is about one-half inch higher than the front. Folders are larger than the papers they contain in order to protect them. Two standard folder sizes are *letter size* for papers that are 8½" x 11" and *legal cap* for papers that are 8½" x 13".

Folders are cut across the top in two ways: so that the back is straight (straight-cut) or so that the back has a tab that projects above the top of the folder. Such tabs bear captions that identify the contents of each folder. Tabs vary in width and position. The tabs of a set of folders that are *one-half cut* are half the width of the folder and have only two positions.

One-third cut folders have three positions, each tab occupying a third of the width of the folder. Another standard tabbing is *one-fifth cut*, which has five positions. There are also folders with *two-fifths cut*, with the tabs in the third and fourth or fourth and fifth positions.

1. Of the following, the BEST title for the above passage is 1.____
   A. Filing Folders
   B. Standard Folder Sizes
   C. The Uses of the Folder
   D. The Use of Tabs

2. According to the above passage, one of the standard folder sizes is called 2.____
   A. Kraft cut
   B. legal cap
   C. one-half cut
   D. straight-cut

3. According to the above passage, tabs are GENERALLY placed along the _____ of the folder. 3.____
   A. back B. front C. left side D. right side

4. According to the above passage, a tab is GENERALLY used to 4.____
   A. distinguish between standard folder sizes
   B. identify the contents of a folder
   C. increase the size of the folder
   D. protect the papers within the folder

5. According to the above passage, a folder that is two-fifths cut has _____ tabs. 5.____
   A. no B. two C. three D. five

6. According to the above passage, one reason for making folders larger than the papers they contain is that 6.____
   A. only a certain size folder can be made from heavy paper
   B. they will protect the papers
   C. they will aid in setting up a tab system
   D. the back of the folder must be higher than the front

Questions 7-15.

DIRECTIONS: Questions 7 through 15 are to be answered SOLELY on the basis of the following passage.

The City University of New York traces its origins to 1847, when the Free Academy, which later became City College, was founded as the first tuition-free municipal college. City and Hunter Colleges were placed under the direction of the Board of Higher Education in 1926, and Brooklyn and Queens Colleges were subsequently added to the system of municipal colleges. In 1955, Staten Island Community College, the first of the two-year colleges sponsored by the Board of Higher Education under the program of the State University of New York, joined the system.

In 1961, the four senior colleges and three community colleges then under the jurisdiction of the Board of Higher Education became the City University of New York, and a University Graduate Division was organized to offer programs leading to the Ph.D. Since then, the university has undergone even more rapid growth. Today, it consists of nine senior colleges, an upper division college which admits students at the junior level, eight community colleges, a graduate division, and an affiliated medical center.

In the summer of 1969, the Board of Higher Education resolved that the time had come to commit the resources of the university to meeting an urgent social need—unrestricted access to higher education for all youths of the City. Determined to prevent the waste of human potential represented by the thousands of high school graduates whose limited educational opportunities left them unable to meet existing admission standards, the Board moved to adopt a policy of Open Admissions. It was their judgment that the best way of determining whether a potential student can benefit from college work is to admit him to college, provide him with the learning assistance he needs, and then evaluate his performance.

Beginning with the class of June 1970, every New York City resident who received a high school diploma from a public or private high school was guaranteed a place in one of the colleges of City University.

7. Of the following, the BEST title for the above passage is 7.____
   A. A Brief History of the City University
   B. High Schools and the City University
   C. The Components of the University
   D. Tuition-free Colleges

8. According to the above passage, which one of the following colleges of the City University was ORIGINALLY called the Free Academy? 8.____
   A. Brooklyn College
   B. City College
   C. Hunter College
   D. Queens College

9. According to the above passage, the system of municipal colleges became the City University of New York in 9.____
A. 1926 B. 1955 C. 1961 D. 1969

10. According to the above passage, Staten Island Community College came under the jurisdiction of the Board of Higher Education 10.____
A. 6 years after a Graduate Division was organized
B. 8 years before the adoption of the Open Admissions Policy
C. 29 years after Brooklyn and Queens Colleges
D. 29 years after City and Hunter Colleges

11. According to the above passage, the Staten Island Community College is 11.____
A. a graduate division center B. a senior college
C. a two-year college D. an upper division college

12. According to the above passage, the TOTAL number of colleges, divisions, and affiliated branches of the City University is 12.____
A. 18 B. 19 C. 20 D. 21

13. According to the above passage, the Open Admissions Policy is designed to determine whether a potential student will benefit from college by PRIMARILY 13.____
A. discouraging competition for placement in the City University among high school students
B. evaluating his performance after entry into college
C. lowering admission standards
D. providing learning assistance before entry into college

14. According to the above passage, the FIRST class to be affected by the Open Admissions Policy was the 14.____
A. high school class which graduated in January 1970
B. City University class which graduated in June 1970
C. high school class when graduated in June 1970
D. City University class when graduated in June 1970

15. According to the above passage, one of the reasons that the Board of Higher Education initiated the policy of Open Admission was to 15.____
A. enable high school graduates with a background of limited educational opportunities to enter college
B. expand the growth of the City University so as to increase the number and variety of degrees offered
C. provide a social resource to the qualified youth of the City
D. revise admission standards to meet the needs of the City

Questions 16-18.

DIRECTIONS: Questions 16 through 18 are to be answered SOLELY on the basis of the following passage.

Hereafter, all probationary students interested in transferring to community college career programs (associate degrees) from liberal arts programs in senior colleges (bachelor degrees) will be eligible for such transfers if they have completed no more than three semesters.

For students with averages 1.5 or above, transfer will be automatic. Those with 1.0 to 1.5 averages can transfer provisionally and will be required to make substantial progress during the first semester in the career program. Once transfer has taken place, only those courses in which passing grades were received will be computed in the community college grade-point average.

No request for transfer will be accepted from probationary students wishing to enter the liberal arts programs at the community college.

16. According to the above passage, the one of the following which is the BEST statement concerning the transfer of probationary students is that a probationary student 16.____
    A. may transfer to a career program at the end of one semester
    B. must complete three semester hours before he is eligible for transfer
    C. is not eligible to transfer to a career program
    D. is eligible to transfer to a liberal arts program

17. Which of the following is the BEST statement of academic evaluation for transfer purposes in the case of probationary students? 17.____
    A. No probationary student with an average under 1.5 may transfer.
    B. A probationary student with an average of 1.3 may not transfer.
    C. A probationary student with an average of 1.6 may transfer.
    D. A probationary student with an average of .8 may transfer on a provisional basis.

18. It is MOST likely that, of the following, the next degree sought by one who already holds the Associate in Science degree would be a(n) _____ degree. 18.____
    A. Assistantship in Science
    B. Associate in Applied Science
    C. Bachelor of Science
    D. Doctor of Philosophy

Questions 19-20.

DIRECTIONS: Questions 19 and 20 are to be answered SOLELY on the basis of the following passage.

Auto: Auto travel requires prior approval by the President and/or appropriate Dean and must be indicated in the *Request for Travel Authorization* form. Employees authorized to use personal autos on official College business will be reimbursed at the rate of 28¢ per mile for the first 500 miles driven and 18¢ per mile for mileage driven in excess of 500 mile. The Comptroller's Office may limit the amount of reimbursement to the expenditure that would have been made if a less expensive mode of transportation (railroad, airplane, bus, etc.) had been utilized. If this occurs, the traveler will have to pick up the excess expenditure as a personal expense.

Tolls, Parking Fees, and Parking Meter Fees are not reimbursable and many not be claimed.

19. Suppose that Professor T gives the office assistant the following memorandum: Used car for official trip to Albany, New York, and return. Distance from New York to Albany is 148 miles. Tolls were $3.50 each way. Parking garage cost $3.00. When preparing the Travel Expense Voucher for Professor T, the figure which should be claimed for transportation is 19.____
   A. $120.88 B. $113.88 C. $82.88 D. $51.44

20. Suppose that Professor V gives the office assistant the following memorandum: Used car for official trip to Pittsburgh, Pennsylvania, and return. Distance from New York to Pittsburgh is 350 miles. Tolls were $3.30, $11.40 going, and $3.30, $2.00 returning. 20.____
   When preparing the Travel Expense Voucher for Professor V, the figure which should be claimed for transportation is
   A. $225.40 B. $176.00 C. $127.40 D. $98.00

Questions 21-25.

DIRECTIONS: Questions 21 through 25 are to be answered SOLELY on the basis of the following passage.

For a period of nearly fifteen years, beginning in the mid-1950's, higher education sustained a phenomenal rate of growth. The factor principally responsible were continuing improvement in the rate of college entrance by high school graduates, a 50 percent increase in the size of the college-age (eighteen to twenty-one) group and—until about 1967—a rapid expansion of university research activity supported by the Federal government.

Today, as one looks ahead to the year 2010, it is apparent that each of these favorable stimuli will either be abated or turn into a negative factor. The rate of growth of the college-age group has already diminished; and from 2000 to 2005, the size of the college-age group has shrunk annually almost as fast as it grew from 1965 to 1970. From 2005 to 2010, this annual decrease will slow down so that by 2010 the age group will be about the same size as it was in 2009. This substantial net decrease in the size of the college-age group (from 1995 to 2010) will dramatically affect college enrollments since, currently, 83 percent of undergraduates are twenty-one and under, and another 11 percent are twenty-to to twenty-four.

21. Which one of the following factors is NOT mentioned in the above passage as contributing to the high rate of growth of higher education? 21.____
   A. A large increase in the size of the eighteen to twenty-one age group
   B. The equalization of educational opportunities among socio-economic groups
   C. The Federal budget impact on research and development spending in the higher education sector
   D. The increasing rate at which high school graduates enter college

22. Based on the information in the above passage, the size of the college-age group in 2010 will be 22.____
    A. larger than it was in 2009
    B. larger than it was in 1995
    C. smaller than it was in 2005
    D. about the same as it was in 2000

23. According to the above passage, the tremendous rate of growth of higher education started around 23.____
    A. 1950
    B. 1955
    C. 1960
    D. 1965

24. The percentage of undergraduates who are over age 24 is MOST NEARLY 24.____
    A. 6%
    B. 8%
    C. 11%
    D. 17%

25. Which one of the following conclusions can be substantiated by the information given in the above passage? 25.____
    A. The college-age group was about the same size in 2000 as it was in 1965.
    B. The annual decrease in the size of the college-age group from 2000 to 2005 is about the same as the annual increase from 1965 to 1970.
    C. The overall decrease in the size of the college-age group from 2000 to 2005 will be followed by an overall increase in its size from 2005 to 2010.
    D. The size of the college-age group is decreasing at a fairly constant rate from1995 to 2010.

KEY (CORRECT ANSWERS)

1.	A	11.	C
2.	B	12.	C
3.	A	13.	B
4.	B	14.	C
5.	B	15.	A
6.	B	16.	A
7.	A	17.	C
8.	B	18.	C
9.	C	19.	C
10.	D	20.	B

21.	B
22.	C
23.	B
24.	A
25.	B

INTERPRETING STATISTICAL DATA GRAPHS, CHARTS, AND TABLES

EXAMINATION SECTION

TEST 1

DIRECTIONS: Each question or incomplete statement is followed by several suggested answers or completions. Select the one that BEST answers the question or completes the statement. *PRINT THE LETTER OF THE CORRECT ANSWER IN THE SPACE AT THE RIGHT.*

Questions 1-5.

DIRECTIONS: Questions 1 through 5 are to be answered SOLELY on the basis of the following table.

ANNUAL SALARIES PAID TO SELECTED CLERICAL TITLES IN FIVE MAJOR CITIES IN 2017 AND 2019

	Clerk	Typist	Steno	Legal Steno	Computer Operator
2019					
Newton	$33,900	$34,800	$36,300	$43,800	$35,400
Barton	$32,400	$34,200	$35,400	$43,500	$24,200
Phelton	$32,400	$32,400	$34,200	$42,000	$33,000
Washburn	$33,600	$34,800	$35,400	$43,800	$34,800
Biltmore	$33,000	$34,200	$35,100	$43,500	$34,500
2017					
Newton	$31,800	$33,600	$35,400	$41,400	$34,500
Barton	$30,000	$31,500	$33,000	$39,600	$31,500
Phelton	$29,400	$30,600	$31,800	$37,800	$31,200
Washburn	$30,600	$32,400	$33,600	$40,200	$32,400
Biltmore	$30,000	$31,800	$33,00	$39,600	$32,100

1. Assume that the value of the fringe benefits offered to clerical employees in 2019 amounted to 14% of their annual salaries in Newton, 17% in Barton, 18% in Phelton, 15% in Washburn, and 16% in Biltmore. The total cost of employing a computer operator for 2019 was GREATEST in 1.____
   A. Newton B. Barton C. Phelton D. Washburn

2. During negotiations for their 2020 contract, the stenographers of Biltmore are demanding that their rate of pay be fixed at 85% of the legal stenographer salary. If this demand is granted and if the legal stenographer salary increases by 7% in 2020, the 2020 stenographer salary will be MOST NEARLY 2.____
   A. $36,972 B. $37,560 C. $39,564 D. $40,020

3. Of the following, the GREATEST percentage increase in salary from 2017 to 2019 was gained by 3.____
   A. clerks in Newton
   B. stenographers in Barton
   C. legal stenographers in Washburn
   D. computer operators in Biltmore

4. The title which achieved the SMALLEST average percentage increase in salary from 2017 to 2019 was 4.____
   A. clerk
   B. typist
   C. stenographer
   D. legal stenographer

5. Assume that, in 2019, clerks accounted for 60% of the clerical work force in Barton. The clerical work force consists of 140 employees. In 2017, the clerks accounted for 65% of the clerical work force in Barton. The clerical work force then consisted of 120 employees. 5.____
   The difference between the 2017 and 2019 payroll for clerks in Barton is MOST NEARLY
   A. $120,000
   B. $240,000
   C. $360,000
   D. $480,000

KEY (CORRECT ANSWERS)

1. A
2. C
3. C
4. C
5. C

TEST 2

DIRECTIONS: Each question or incomplete statement is followed by several suggested answers or completions. Select the one that BEST answers the question or completes the statement. *PRINT THE LETTER OF THE CORRECT ANSWER IN THE SPACE AT THE RIGHT.*

Questions 1-9.

DIRECTIONS: Questions 1 through 9 are to be answered SOLELY on the basis of the facts given in the following table, which contains certain information about employees in a city bureau.

RECORD OF EMPLOYEES IN A CITY BUREAU					
NAME	TITLE	AGE	ANNUAL SALARY	YEARS OF SERVICE	EXAMINATION RATING
Jones	Clerk	34	$40,800	10	82
Smith	Stenographer	25	$38,400	2	72
Black	Typist	19	$28,800	1	71
Brown	Stenographer	36	$50,400	12	88
Thomas	Accountant	49	$82,400	21	91
Gordon	Clerk	31	$60,000	8	81
Johnson	Stenographer	26	$52,800	5	75
White	Accountant	53	$72,000	30	90
Spencer	Clerk	42	$55,200	19	85
Taylor	Typist	24	$43,200	5	74
Simpson	Accountant	37	$100,000	1	87
Reid	Typist	20	$24,000	2	72
Fulton	Accountant	55	$110,000	31	100
Chambers	Clerk	22	$31,200	4	75
Calhoun	Stenographer	48	$57,600	16	80

1. The name of the employee whose salary would be the middle one if all the salaries were ranked in order of magnitude is 1.____
   A. White B. Johnson C. Brown D. Spencer

2. The combined monthly salary of all the stenographers EXCEEDS the combined monthly salary of all the clerks by 2.____
   A. $12,000 B. $1,000 C. $45,600 D. $1,200

3. The age of the employee who received the HIGHEST rating in the examination among those who have less than 10 years of service is _____ years. 3.____
   A. 22 B. 31 C. 55 D. 34

4. The average examination rating of those employees who had 15 years of service or more as compared with the average examination rating of those employees who had 5 years of service or less is MOST NEARLY _____ points _____. 4.____

A. 16; greater B. 7; greater C. 10; less D. 25; greater

5. The name of the youngest employee whose monthly salary is more than $2,000 per month and who has more than one year of service is 5.____

A. Reid B. Black C. Chambers D. Taylor

6. The name of the employee who received an examination rating of over 85%, who has more than 15 years of service, and who earns a yearly salary of more than $50,000 but less than $80,000 is 6.____

A. Thomas B. Spencer C. Calhoun D. White

7. The annual salary of the HIGHEST paid stenographer is 7.____

A. more than twice as great as the salary of the youngest employee
B. greater than the salary of the oldest typist but not as great as the salary of the oldest clerk
C. greater than the salary of the highest paid typist but not as great as the salary of the lowest paid accountant
D. less than the combined salaries of the two youngest typists

8. The number of employees whose annual salary is more than $31,200 but less than $57,600 and who have at least 5 years of service is 8.____

A. 11 B. 8 C. 6 D. 5

9. Of the following, it would be MOST accurate to state that the 9.____

A. youngest employee is lowest with respect to number of years of service, examination rating, and salary
B. oldest employee is highest with respect to number of years of service, examination rating, but not with respect to salary
C. annual salary of the youngest clerk is $2,400 more than the annual salary of the youngest typist and $4,800 less than the annual salary of the youngest stenographer
D. difference in age between the youngest and oldest typist is less than one-fourth the difference in age between the youngest and oldest stenographer

KEY (CORRECT ANSWERS)

1.	B	6.	D
2.	B	7.	C
3.	B	8.	D
4.	A	9.	D
5.	C		

TEST 3

DIRECTIONS: Each question or incomplete statement is followed by several suggested answers or completions. Select the one that BEST answers the question or completes the statement. *PRINT THE LETTER OF THE CORRECT ANSWER IN THE SPACE AT THE RIGHT.*

Questions 1-10.

DIRECTIONS: Questions 1 through 10 are to be answered SOLELY on the basis of the Personnel Record of Division X shown below.

DIVISION X
PERSONNEL RECORD – CURRENT YEAR

				No. of Days Absent		
Employee	Bureau in Which Employed	Title	Annual Salary	On Vacation	On Sick Leave	No. of Times Late
Abbot	Mail	Clerk	$31,200	18	0	1
Barnes	Mail	Clerk	$25,200	25	3	7
Davis	Mail	Typist	$24,000	21	9	2
Adams	Payroll	Accountant	$42,500	10	0	2
Bell	Payroll	Bookkeeper	$31,200	23	2	5
Duke	Payroll	Clerk	$27,600	24	4	3
Gross	Payroll	Clerk	$21,600	12	5	7
Lane	Payroll	Stenographer	$26,400	19	16	20
Reed	Payroll	Typist	$22,800	15	11	11
Arnold	Record	Clerk	$32,400	6	15	9
Cane	Record	Clerk	$24,500	14	3	4
Fay	Record	Clerk	$21,100	20	0	4
Hale	Record	Typist	$25,200	18	2	7
Baker	Supply	Clerk	$30,000	20	3	2
Clark	Supply	Clerk	$27,600	25	6	5
Ford	Supply	Typist	$22,800	25	4	22

1. The percentage of the total number of employees who are clerks is MOST NEARLY 1.____
   A. 25% B. 33% C. 38% D. 56%

2. Of the following employees, the one who receives a monthly salary of $2,100 is 2.____
   A. Barnes B. Gross C. Reed D. Clark

3. The difference between the annual salary of the highest paid clerk and that of the lowest paid clerk is 3.____
   A. $6,000 B. $8,400 C. $11,300 D. $20,900

4. The number of employees receiving more than $25,000 a year but less than $40,000 a year is 4.____
   A. 6 B. 9 C. 12 D. 15

5. The TOTAL annual salary of the employees of the Mail Bureau is _____ the total annual salary of the employees of the _____. 5.____
   A. one-half of; Payroll Bureau
   B. less than; Record Bureau by $21,600
   C. equal to; Supply Bureau
   D. less than; Payroll Bureau by $71,600

6. The average annual salary of the employees who are not clerks is MOST NEARLY 6.____
   A. $23,700 B. $25,450 C. $26,800 D. $27,850

7. If all the employees were given a 10% increase in pay, the annual salary of Lane would then be 7.____
   A. *greater* than that of Barnes by $1,320
   B. *less* than that of Bell by $4,280
   C. *equal to* that of Clark
   D. *greater* than that of Ford by $3,600

8. Of the clerks who earned less than $30,000 a year, the one who was late the FEWEST number of times was late _____ time(s). 8.____
   A. 1 B. 2 C. 3 D. 4

9. The bureau in which the employees were late the FEWEST number of times on an average is the _____ Bureau. 9.____
   A. Mail B. Payroll C. Record D. Supply

10. The MOST accurate of the following statements is that 10.____
    A. Reed was late more often than any other typist
    B. Bell took more time off for vacation than any other employee earning $30,000 or more annually
    C. of the typists, Ford was the one who was absent the fewest number of times because of sickness
    D. three clerks took no time off because of sickness

KEY (CORRECT ANSWERS)

1.	D	6.	D
2.	A	7.	A
3.	C	8.	C
4.	B	9.	A
5.	C	10.	B

TEST 4

DIRECTIONS: Each question or incomplete statement is followed by several suggested answers or completions. Select the one that BEST answers the question or completes the statement. *PRINT THE LETTER OF THE CORRECT ANSWER IN THE SPACE AT THE RIGHT.*

Questions 1-10.

DIRECTIONS: Questions 1 through 10 are to be answered SOLELY on the basis of the Weekly Payroll Record shown below of Bureau X in a public agency. In answering these questions, note that gross weekly salary is the salary before deductions have been made; take-home pay is the amount remaining after all indicated weekly deductions have been made from the gross weekly salary. In answering questions involving annual amounts, compute on the basis of 52 weeks per year.

BUREAU X
WEEKLY PAYROLL PERIOD

Unit in Which Employed	Employee	Title	Gross Weekly Salary (Before Deductions)	Weekly Deductions From Gross Salary		
				Medical Insurance	Income Tax	Pension System
Accounting	Allen	Accountant	$950	$14.50	$125.00	$53.20
Accounting	Barth	Bookkeeper	$720	$19.00	$62.00	$40.70
Accounting	Keller	Clerk	$580	$6.50	$82.00	$33.10
Accounting	Peters	Typist	$560	$6.50	$79.00	$35.30
Accounting	Simons	Stenographer	$610	$14.50	$64.00	$37.80
Information	Brown	Clerk	$560	$13.00	$56.00	$42.20
Information	Smith	Clerk	$590	$14.50	$61.00	$58.40
Information	Turner	Typist	$580	$13.00	$59.00	$62.60
Information	Williams	Stenographer	$620	$19.00	$44.00	$69.40
Mail	Conner	Clerk	$660	$13.00	$74.00	$55.40
Mail	Farrell	Typist	$540	$6.50	$75.00	$34.00
Mail	Johnson	Stenographer	$580	$19.00	$36.00	$37.10
Records	Dillon	Clerk	$640	$6.50	$94.00	$58.20
Records	Martin	Clerk	$540	$19.00	$29.00	$50.20
Records	Standish	Typist	$620	$14.50	$67.00	$60.10
Records	Wilson	Stenographer	$690	$6.50	$101.00	$75.60

1. Dillon's annual take-home pay is MOST NEARLY 1.____
   A. $25,000 B. $27,000 C. $31,000 D. $33,000

2. The difference between Turner's gross annual salary and his annual take-home pay is MOST NEARLY 2.____
   A. $3,000 B. $5,000 C. $7,000 D. $9,000

3. Of the following, the employee whose weekly take-home pay is CLOSEST to that of Keller's is 3.____
   A. Peters B. Brown C. Smith D. Turner

4. The average gross annual salary of the typists is 4.____
   A. less than $27,500
   B. more than $27,500 but less than $30,000
   C. more than $30,000 but less than $32,500
   D. more than $32,500

5. The average gross weekly salary of the stenographers EXCEEDS the gross weekly salary of the clerk by 5.____
   A. $20 B. $30 C. $40 D. $50

6. Of the following employees in Accounting Unit, the one who pays the HIGHEST percentage of his gross weekly salary for the Pension System is 6.____
   A. Barth B. Keller C. Peters D. Simons

7. For all of the Accounting Unit employees, the total annual deductions for Medical Insurance are less than the total annual deductions for the Pension System by MOST NEARLY 7.____
   A. $6,000 B. $7,000 C. $8,000 D. $9,000

8. Of the following, the employee whose total weekly deductions are MOST NEARLY 27% of his gross weekly salary is 8.____
   A. Barth B. Brown C. Martin D. Wilson

9. The total amount of the gross weekly salaries of all the employees in the Records Unit is MOST NEARLY 9.____
   A. 95% of the total amount of the gross weekly salaries of all the employees in the Information Unit
   B. 10% greater than the total amount of the gross weekly salaries of all the employees in the Mail Unit
   C. 75% of the total amount of the gross weekly salaries of all the employees in the Accounting Unit
   D. four times as great as the total amount deducted weekly for tax for all the employees in the Records Unit

10. For the employees in the Information Unit, the AVERAGE weekly deductions for Income Tax _____ the average weekly deduction for _____. 10.____
   A. exceeds; Income Tax for the employees in the Records Unit
   B. is less than; the Pension System for the employees in the Mail Unit
   C. exceeds; Income Tax for the employees in the Accounting Unit
   D. is less than; the Pension System for the employees in the Records Unit

KEY (CORRECT ANSWERS)

1.	A	6.	C
2.	C	7.	B
3.	C	8.	D
4.	B	9.	C
5.	B	10.	D

TEST 5

DIRECTIONS: Each question or incomplete statement is followed by several suggested answers or completions. Select the one that BEST answers the question or completes the statement. *PRINT THE LETTER OF THE CORRECT ANSWER IN THE SPACE AT THE RIGHT.*

Questions 1-9.

DIRECTIONS: Questions 1 through 9 are to be answered SOLELY on the basis of the following information.

Assume that the following rules for computing service ratings are to be used experimentally in determining service ratings of seven permanent city employees. (Note that these rules are hypothetical and are NOT to be confused with the existing method of computing service ratings for city employees). The personnel record of each of these seven employees is given in Table II. You are to determine the answer to each of the questions on the basis of the rules given below for computing service ratings and the data contained in the personnel records of these seven employees.

All computations should be made as of the close of the rating period ending March 31, 2017.

Service Rating

The service rating of each permanent competitive class employee shall be computed by adding the following three scores: (1) a basic score, (2) the employee's seniority score, and (3) the employee's efficiency score.

Seniority Score

An employee's seniority score shall be computed by crediting him with ½% per year for each year of service starting with the date of the employee's entrance as a permanent employee into the competitive class, up to a maximum of 15 years (7½%).

A residual fractional period of eight months or more shall be considered as a full year and credited with ½%. A residual fraction of from four to, but not including, eight months shall be considered as half-year and credited with ¼%. A residual fraction of less than four months shall receive no credit in the seniority score.

For example, a person who entered the competitive class as a permanent employee on August 1, 2014 would, as of March 31, 2017, be credited with a seniority score of 1½% for his 2 years and 8 months of service.

Efficiency Score

An employee's efficiency score shall be computed by adding the annual efficiency ratings received by him during his service in his present position. (Where there are negative efficiency ratings, such ratings shall be subtracted from the sum of the positive efficiency ratings.) An employee's annual efficiency rating shall be based on the grade he receives from his supervisor for his work performance during the annual efficiency rating period.

Basic Score

A basic score of 70% shall be given to each employee upon permanent appointment to a competitive class position.

An employee shall receive a grade of A for performing work of the highest quality and shall be credited with an efficiency rating of plus (+)3%. An employee shall receive a grade of F for performing work of the lowest quality and shall receive an efficiency rating of minus (-)2%. Table I, entitled BASS FOR DETERMINING ANNUAL EFFICIENCY RATINGS, lists the six grades of work performance with their equivalent annual efficiency ratings. Table I also lists the efficiency ratings to be assigned for service in a position for less than a year during the annual efficiency rating period.

The annual efficiency rating period shall run from April 1 to March 31, inclusive.

TABLE I – BASIS FOR DETERMINING ANNUAL EFFICIENCY RATINGS				
			Annual Efficiency Rating for Service in a Position For	
Quality of Work Performed	Grade Assigned	8 Months to a Full Year	At Least 4 Months But Less Than 8 Months	Less Than 4 Months
Highest	A	+3%	+1½%	0%
Good	B	+2%	+1%	0%
Standard	C	+1%	+ ½%	0%
Substandard	D	0%	0%	0%
Poor	E	-1%	-4%	0%
Lowest	F	-2%	-1%	0%

Appointment or Promotion During an Efficiency Rating Period

An employee who has been appointed or promoted during an efficiency rating period shall receive for that period an efficiency rating only for work performed by him during the portion of the period that he served in the position to which he was appointed or promoted. His efficiency rating for the period shall be determined in accordance with Table I.

Sample Computation of Service Rating

John Smith entered the competitive class as a permanent employee on December 1, 2012 and was promoted to his present position as a Clerk, Grade 3, on November 1, 2015. As a Clerk, Grade 3, he received a grade of B for work performed during the five-month period extending from November 1, 2015 to March 31, 2016 and a grade of C for work performed during the full annual period extending from April 1, 2016 to March 31, 2017.

On the basis of the RULES FOR COMPUTING SERVICE RATINGS, John Smith should be credited with:

70% Basic Score
2¼% Seniority Score – for 4 years and 4 months of service (from 12/1/12 to 3/31/17)
2% Efficiency Score – for 5 months of B service and a full _____ year of C service
74¼%

TABLE II
PERSONNEL RECORD OF SEVEN PERMANENT
COMPETITIVE CLASS EMPLOYEES

Employee	Present Position	Date of Appointment or Promotion to Present Position	Date of Entry as Permanent Employment in Competitive Class
Allen	Clerk, Gr. 5	6-1-13	7-1-00
Brown	Clerk, Gr. 4	1-1-15	7-1-17
Cole	Clerk, Gr. 3	9-1-13	11-1-10
Fox	Clerk, Gr. 3	10-1-13	9-1-08
Green	Clerk, Gr. 2	12-1-11	12-1-11
Hunt	Clerk, Gr. 2	7-1-12	7-1-12
Kane	Steno, Gr. 3	11-16-14	3-1-11

GRADES RECEIVED ANNUALLY FOR WORK
PERFORMED IN PRESENT POSITION

Employee	4-1-11 to 3-31-12	4-1-12 to 3-31-13	4-1-13 to 3-31-14	4-1-14 to 3-31-15	4-1-15 to 3-31-16	4-1-16 to 3-31-17
Allen			C*	C	B	C
Brown				C*	C	B
Cole			A*	B	C	C
Fox			C*	C	D	C
Green	C*	D	C	D	C	C
Hunt		C*	C	E	C	C
Kane				B*	B	C

EXPLANATORY NOTES
* Served in present position for less than a full year during this rating period. (Note date of appointment, or promotion, to present position.)
All seven employees have served continuously as permanent employees since their entry into the competitive class.

Questions 1 through 9 refer to the employees listed in Table II. You are to answer these questions SOLELY on the basis of the preceding RULES FOR COMPUTING SERVICE RATINGS and on the information concerning these seven employees given in Table II. You are reminded that all computations are to be made as of the close of the rating period ending March 31, 2017. Candidates may find it helpful to arrange their computations on their scratch paper in an orderly manner since the computations for one question may also be utilized in answering another question.

1. The seniority score of Allen is 1.____
   A. 7½% B. 8½% C. 8% D. 8¼%

2. The seniority score of Fox EXCEEDS that of Cole by 2.____
   A. 1½% B. 2% C. 1% D. ¾%

3. The seniority score of Brown is 3.____
   A. *equal* to Hunt's
   B. *twice* Hunt's
   C. *more* than Hunt's by 1½%
   D. *less* than by Hunt's by ½%

4. Green's efficiency score is 4.____
   A. *twice* that of Kane
   B. *equal* to that of Kane
   C. *less* than Kane's by ½%
   D. *less* than Kane's by 1%

5. Of the following employees, the one who has the LOWEST efficiency score is 5.____
   A. Brown B. Fox C. Hunt D. Kane

6. A comparison of Hunt's efficiency score with his seniority score reveals that his efficiency score is 6.____
   A. *less* than his seniority score by ½%
   B. *less* than his seniority score by ¾%
   C. *equal* to his seniority score
   D. *greater* than his seniority score by ½%

7. Fox's service rating is 7.____
   A. 72½% B. 74% C. 76½% D. 76¾%

8. Brown's service rating is 8.____
   A. less than 78%
   B. 78%
   C. 78¼%
   D. more than 78¼%

9. Cole's service rating EXCEEDS Kane's by 9.____
   A. less than 2%
   B. 2%
   C. 2¼%
   D. more than 2¼%

KEY (CORRECT ANSWERS)

1.	A	6.	D
2.	C	7.	D
3.	B	8.	B
4.	C	9.	A
5.	B		

PHILOSOPHY, PRINCIPLES, PRACTICES, AND TECHNICS
OF
SUPERVISION, ADMINISTRATION, MANAGEMENT, AND ORGANIZATION

TABLE OF CONTENTS

PHILOSOPHY, PRINCIPLES, PRACTICES, AND TECHNICS
OF
SUPERVISION, ADMINISTRATION, MANAGEMENT, AND ORGANIZATION

MEANING OF SUPERVISION

The extension of the democratic philosophy has been accompanied by an extension in the scope of supervision. Modern leaders and supervisors no longer think of supervision in the narrow sense of being confined chiefly to visiting employees, supplying materials, or rating the staff. They regard supervision as being intimately related to all the concerned agencies of society, they speak of the supervisor's function in terms of "growth," rather than the "improvement" of employees.

This modern concept of supervision may be defined as follows: Supervision is leadership and the development of leadership within groups which are cooperatively engaged in inspection, research, training, guidance, and evaluation.

THE OLD AND THE NEW SUPERVISION

<u>TRADITIONAL</u>

1. Inspection
2. Focused on the employee
3. Visitation
4. Random and haphazard
5. Imposed and authoritarian
6. One person usually

<u>MODERN</u>

1. Study and analysis
2. Focused on aims, materials, methods, supervisors, employees, environment
3. Demonstrations, intervisitation, workshops, directed reading, bulletins, etc.
4. Definitely organized and planned (scientific)
5. Cooperative and democratic
6. Many persons involved (creative)

THE EIGHT (8) BASIC PRINCIPLES OF THE NEW SUPERVISION

I. Principle of Responsibility
Authority to act and responsibility for acting must be joined.
   A. If you give responsibility, give authority.
   B. Define employee duties clearly.
   C. Protect employees from criticism by others.
   D. Recognize the rights as well as obligations of employees.
   E. Achieve the aims of a democratic society insofar as it is possible within the area of your work.
   F. Establish a situation favorable to training and learning.
   G. Accept ultimate responsibility for everything done in your section, unit, office, division, department.
   H. Good administration and good supervision are inseparable.

II. Principle of Authority
The success of the supervisor is measured by the extent to which the power of authority is not used.
A. Exercise simplicity and informality in supervision
B. Use the simplest machinery of supervision
C. If it is good for the organization as a whole, it is probably justified.
D. Seldom be arbitrary or authoritative.
E. Do not base your work on the power of position or of personality.
F. Permit and encourage the free expression of opinions.

III. Principle of Self-Growth
The success of the supervisor is measured by the extent to which, and the speed with which, he is no longer needed.
A. Base criticism on principles, not on specifics.
B. Point out higher activities to employees.
C. Train for self-thinking by employees to meet new situations.
D. Stimulate initiative, self-reliance, and individual responsibility
E. Concentrate on stimulating the growth of employees rather than on removing defects.

IV. Principle of Individual Worth
Respect for the individual is a paramount consideration in supervision.
A. Be human and sympathetic in dealing with employees.
B. Don't nag about things to be done.
C. Recognize the individual differences among employees and seek opportunities to permit best expression of each personality.

V. Principle of Creative Leadership
The best supervision is that which is not apparent to the employee.
A. Stimulate, don't drive employees to creative action.
B. Emphasize doing good things.
C. Encourage employees to do what they do best.
D. Do not be too greatly concerned with details of subject or method.
E. Do not be concerned exclusively with immediate problems and activities.
F. Reveal higher activities and make them both desired and maximally possible.
G. Determine procedures in the light of each situation but see that these are derived from a sound basic philosophy.
H. Aid, inspire, and lead so as to liberate the creative spirit latent in all good employees.

VI. Principle of Success and Failure
There are no unsuccessful employees, only unsuccessful supervisors who have failed to give proper leadership.
A. Adapt suggestions to the capacities, attitudes, and prejudices of employees.
B. Be gradual, be progressive, be persistent.
C. Help the employee find the general principle; have the employee apply his own problem to the general principle.
D. Give adequate appreciation for good work and honest effort.
E. Anticipate employee difficulties and help to prevent them.
F. Encourage employees to do the desirable things they will do anyway.
G. Judge your supervision by the results it secures.

VII. Principle of Science
Successful supervision is scientific, objective, and experimental. It is based on facts, not on prejudices.
A. Be cumulative in results.
B. Never divorce your suggestions from the goals of training.
C. Don't be impatient of results.
D. Keep all matters on a professional, not a personal, level.
E. Do not be concerned exclusively with immediate problems and activities.
F. Use objective means of determining achievement and rating where possible.

VIII. Principle of Cooperation
Supervision is a cooperative enterprise between supervisor and employee.
A. Begin with conditions as they are.
B. Ask opinions of all involved when formulating policies.
C. Organization is as good as its weakest link.
D. Let employees help to determine policies and department programs.
E. Be approachable and accessible—physically and mentally.
F. Develop pleasant social relationships.

WHAT IS ADMINISTRATION

Administration is concerned with providing the environment, the material facilities, and the operational procedures that will promote the maximum growth and development of supervisors and employees. (Organization is an aspect and a concomitant of administration.)

There is no sharp line of demarcation between supervision and administration; these functions are intimately interrelated and, often, overlapping. They are complementary activities.

I. Practices Commonly Classed as "Supervisory"
A. Conducting employees' conferences
B. Visiting sections, units, offices, divisions, departments
C. Arranging for demonstrations
D. Examining plans
E. Suggesting professional reading
F. Interpreting bulletins
G. Recommending in-service training courses
H. Encouraging experimentation
I. Appraising employee morale
J. Providing for intervisitation

II. Practices Commonly Classified as "Administrative"
A. Management of the office
B. Arrangement of schedules for extra duties
C. Assignment of rooms or areas
D. Distribution of supplies
E. Keeping records and reports
F. Care of audio-visual materials
G. Keeping inventory records
H. Checking record cards and books

I. Programming special activities
J. Checking on the attendance and punctuality of employees

III. Practices Commonly Classified as Both "Supervisory" and "Administrative"
   A. Program construction
   B. Testing or evaluating outcomes
   C. Personnel accounting
   D. Ordering instructional materials

RESPONSIBILITIES OF THE SUPERVISOR

A person employed in a supervisory capacity must constantly be able to improve his own efficiency and ability. He represent the employer to the employees and only continuous self-examination can make him a capable supervisor.

Leadership and training are the supervisor's responsibility. An efficient working unit is one in which the employees work with the supervisor. It is his job to bring out the best in his employees. He must always be relaxed, courteous, and calm in his association with his employees. Their feelings are important, and a harsh attitude does not develop the most efficient employees.

COMPETENCES OF THE SUPERVISOR

I. Complete knowledge of the duties and responsibilities of his position.
II. To be able to organize a job, plan ahead, and carry through.
III. To have self-confidence and initiative.
IV. To be able to handle the unexpected situation and make quick decisions.
V. To be able to properly train subordinates in the positions they are best suited for.
VI. To be able to keep good human relations among his subordinates.
VII. To be able to keep good human relations between his subordinates and himself and to earn their respect and trust.

THE PROFESSIONAL SUPERVISOR-EMPLOYEE RELATIONSHIP

There are two kinds of efficiency: one kind is only apparent and is produced in organizations through the exercise of mere discipline; this is but a simulation of the second, or true, efficiency which springs from spontaneous cooperation. If you are a manager, no matter how great or small your responsibility, it is your job, in the final analysis, to create and develop this involuntary cooperation among the people whom you supervise. For, no matter how powerful a combination of money, machines, and materials a company may have, this is a dead and sterile thing without a team of willing, thinking, and articulate people to guide it.

The following 21 points are presented as indicative of the exemplary basic relationship that should exist between supervisor and employee:

1. Each person wants to be liked and respected by his fellow employee and wants to be treated with consideration and respect by his superior.
2. The most competent employee will make an error. However, in a unit where good relations exist between the supervisor and his employees, tenseness and fear do not exist. Thus, errors are not hidden or covered up, and the efficiency of a unit is not impaired.

3. Subordinates resent rules, regulations, or orders that are unreasonable or unexplained.
4. Subordinates are quick to resent unfairness, harshness, injustices, and favoritism.
5. An employee will accept responsibility if he knows that he will be complimented for a job well done, and not too harshly chastised for failure; that his supervisor will check the cause of the failure, and, if it was the supervisor's fault, he will assume the blame therefore. If it was the employee's fault, his supervisor will explain the correct method or means of handling the responsibility.
6. An employee wants to receive credit for a suggestion he has made, that is used. If a suggestion cannot be used, the employee is entitled to an explanation. The supervisor should not say "no" and close the subject.
7. Fear and worry slow up a worker's ability. Poor working environment can impair his physical and mental health. A good supervisor avoids forceful methods, threats, and arguments to get a job done.
8. A forceful supervisor is able to train his employees individually and as a team, and is able to motivate them in the proper channels.
9. A mature supervisor is able to properly evaluate his subordinates and to keep them happy and satisfied.
10. A sensitive supervisor will never patronize his subordinates.
11. A worthy supervisor will respect his employees' confidences.
12. Definite and clear-cut responsibilities should be assigned to each executive.
13. Responsibility should always be coupled with corresponding authority.
14. No change should be made in the scope or responsibilities of a position without a definite understanding to that effect on the part of all persons concerned.
15. No executive or employee, occupying a single position in the organization, should be subject to definite orders from more than one source.
16. Orders should never be given to subordinates over the head of a responsible executive. Rather than do this, the officer in question should be supplanted.
17. Criticisms of subordinates should, whoever possible, be made privately, and in no case should a subordinate be criticized in the presence of executives or employees of equal or lower rank.
18. No dispute or difference between executives or employees as to authority or responsibilities should be considered too trivial for prompt and careful adjudication.
19. Promotions, wage changes, and disciplinary action should always be approved by the executive immediately superior to the one directly responsible.
20. No executive or employee should ever be required, or expected, to be at the same time an assistant to, and critic of, another.
21. Any executive whose work is subject to regular inspection should, wherever practicable, be given the assistance and facilities necessary to enable him to maintain an independent check of the quality of his work.

MINI-TEXT IN SUPERVISION, ADMINISTRATION, MANAGEMENT, AND ORGANIZATION

I. Brief Highlights

Listed concisely and sequentially are major headings and important data in the field for quick recall and review.

A. Levels of Management

Any organization of some size has several levels of management. In terms of a ladder, the levels are:

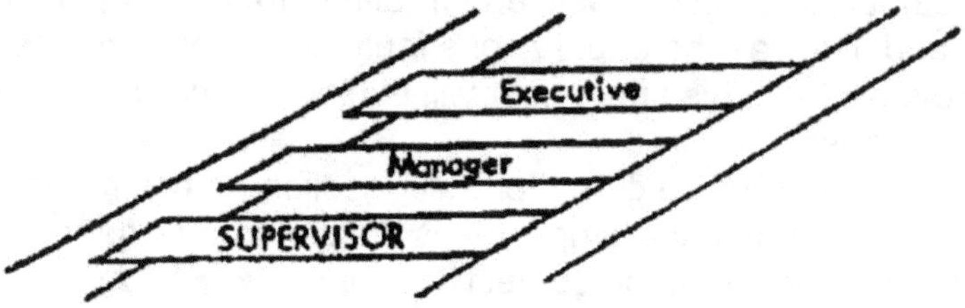

The first level is very important because it is the beginning point of management leadership.

B. What the Supervisor Must Learn

A supervisor must learn to:

1. Deal with people and their differences
2. Get the job done through people
3. Recognize the problems when they exist
4. Overcome obstacles to good performance
5. Evaluate the performance of people
6. Check his own performance in terms of accomplishment

C. A Definition of Supervisor

The term supervisor means any individual having authority, in the interests of the employer, to hire, transfer, suspend, lay-off, recall, promote, discharge, assign, reward, or discipline other employees or responsibility to direct them, or to adjust their grievances, or effectively to recommend such action, if, in connection with the foregoing, exercise of such authority is not of a merely routine or clerical nature but requires the use of independent judgment.

D. Elements of the Team Concept

What is involved in teamwork? The component parts are:

1. Members
2. A leader
3. Goals
4. Plans
5. Cooperation
6. Spirit

E. Principles of Organization

1. A team member must know what his job is.
2. Be sure that the nature and scope of a job are understood.
3. Authority and responsibility should be carefully spelled out.
4. A supervisor should be permitted to make the maximum number of decisions affecting his employees.
5. Employees should report to only one supervisor.
6. A supervisor should direct only as many employees as he can handle effectively.
7. An organization plan should be flexible.

8. Inspection and performance of work should be separate.
9. Organizational problems should receive immediate attention.
10. Assign work in line with ability and experience.

F. The Four Important Parts of Every Job

1. Inherent in every job is the *accountability* for results.
2. A second set of factors in every job is *responsibilities*.
3. Along with duties and responsibilities one must have the *authority* to act within certain limits without obtaining permission to proceed.
4. No job exists in a vacuum. The supervisor is surrounded by key *relationships*.

G. Principles of Delegation

Where work is delegated for the first time, the supervisor should think in terms of these questions:

1. Who is best qualified to do this?
2. Can an employee improve his abilities by doing this?
3. How long should an employee spend on this?
4. Are there any special problems for which he will need guidance?
5. How broad a delegation can I make?

H. Principles of Effective Communications

1. Determine the media.
2. To whom directed?
3. Identification and source authority.
4. Is communication understood?

I. Principles of Work Improvement

1. Most people usually do only the work which is assigned to them.
2. Workers are likely to fit assigned work into the time available to perform it.
3. A good workload usually stimulates output.
4. People usually do their best work when they know that results will be reviewed or inspected.
5. Employees usually feel that someone else is responsible for conditions of work, workplace layout, job methods, type of tools/equipment, and other such factors.
6. Employees are usually defensive about their job security.
7. Employees have natural resistance to change.
8. Employees can support or destroy a supervisor.
9. A supervisor usually earns the respect of his people through his personal example of diligence and efficiency.

J. Areas of Job Improvement

The areas of job improvement are quite numerous, but the most common ones which a supervisor can identify and utilize are:

1. Departmental layout
2. Flow of work
3. Workplace layout
4. Utilization of manpower
5. Work methods
6. Materials handling

7. Utilization
8. Motion economy

K. Seven Key Points in Making Improvements
1. Select the job to be improved
2. Study how it is being done now
3. Question the present method
4. Determine actions to be taken
5. Chart proposed method
6. Get approval and apply
7. Solicit worker participation

I. Corrective Techniques of Job Improvement
Specific Problems
1. Size of workload
2. Inability to meet schedules
3. Strain and fatigue
4. Improper use of men and skills
5. Waste, poor quality, unsafe conditions
6. Bottleneck conditions that hinder output
7. Poor utilization of equipment and machine
8. Efficiency and productivity of labor

General Improvement
1. Departmental layout
2. Flow of work
3. Work plan layout
4. Utilization of manpower
5. Work methods
6. Materials handling
7. Utilization of equipment
8. Motion economy

Corrective Techniques
1. Study with scale model
2. Flow chart study
3. Motion analysis
4. Comparison of units produced to standard allowance
5. Methods analysis
6. Flow chart and equipment study
7. Down time vs. running time
8. Motion analysis

M. A Planning Checklist
1. Objectives
2. Controls
3. Delegations
4. Communications
5. Resources
6. Manpower

7. Equipment
8. Supplies and materials
9. Utilization of time
10. Safety
11. Money
12. Work
13. Timing of improvements

N. Five Characteristics of Good Directions

In order to get results, directions must be:

1. Possible of accomplishment
2. Agreeable with worker interests
3. Related to mission
4. Planned and complete
5. Unmistakably clear

O. Types of Directions

1. Demands or direct orders
2. Requests
3. Suggestion or implication
4. volunteering

P. Controls

A typical listing of the overall areas in which the supervisor should establish controls might be:

1. Manpower
2. Materials
3. Quality of work
4. Quantity of work
5. Time
6. Space
7. Money
8. Methods

Q. Orienting the New Employee

1. Prepare for him
2. Welcome the new employee
3. Orientation for the job
4. Follow-up

R. Checklist for Orienting New Employees

	Yes	No
1. Do you appreciate the feelings of new employees when they first report for work?	___	___
2. Are you aware of the fact that the new employee must make a big adjustment to his job?	___	___
3. Have you given him good reasons for liking the job and the organization?	___	___
4. Have you prepared for his first day on the job?	___	___
5. Did you welcome him cordially and make him feel needed?	___	___

		Yes	No
6.	Did you establish rapport with him so that he feels free to talk and discuss matters with you?	___	___
7.	Did you explain his job to him and his relationship to you?	___	___
8.	Does he know that his work will be evaluated periodically on a basis that is fair and objective?	___	___
9.	Did you introduce him to his fellow workers in such a way that they are likely to accept him?	___	___
10.	Does he know what employee benefits he will receive?	___	___
11.	Does he understand the importance of being on the job and what to do if he must leave his duty station?	___	___
12.	Has he been impressed with the importance of accident prevention and safe practice?	___	___
13.	Does he generally know his way around the department?	___	___
14.	Is he under the guidance of a sponsor who will teach the right way of doing things?	___	___
15.	Do you plan to follow-up so that he will continue to adjust successfully to his job?	___	___

S. Principles of Learning
1. Motivation
2. Demonstration or explanation
3. Practice

T. Causes of Poor Performance
1. Improper training for job
2. Wrong tools
3. Inadequate directions
4. Lack of supervisory follow-up
5. Poor communications
6. Lack of standards of performance
7. Wrong work habits
8. Low morale
9. Other

U. Four Major Steps in On-The-Job Instruction
1. Prepare the worker
2. Present the operation
3. Tryout performance
4. Follow-up

V. Employees Want Five Things
1. Security
2. Opportunity
3. Recognition
4. Inclusion
5. Expression

W. Some Don'ts in Regard to Praise

1. Don't praise a person for something he hasn't done.
2. Don't praise a person unless you can be sincere.
3. Don't be sparing in praise just because your superior withholds it from you.
4. Don't let too much time elapse between good performance and recognition of it

X. How to Gain Your Workers' Confidence

Methods of developing confidence include such things as:

1. Knowing the interests, habits, hobbies of employees
2. Admitting your own inadequacies
3. Sharing and telling of confidence in others
4. Supporting people when they are in trouble
5. Delegating matters that can be well handled
6. Being frank and straightforward about problems and working conditions
7. Encouraging others to bring their problems to you
8. Taking action on problems which impede worker progress

Y. Sources of Employee Problems

On-the-job causes might be such things as:

1. A feeling that favoritism is exercised in assignments
2. Assignment of overtime
3. An undue amount of supervision
4. Changing methods or systems
5. Stealing of ideas or trade secrets
6. Lack of interest in job
7. Threat of reduction in force
8. Ignorance or lack of communications
9. Poor equipment
10. Lack of knowing how supervisor feels toward employee
11. Shift assignments

Off-the-job problems might have to do with:

1. Health
2. Finances
3. Housing
4. Family

Z. The Supervisor's Key to Discipline

There are several key points about discipline which the supervisor should keep in mind:

1. Job discipline is one of the disciplines of life and is directed by the supervisor.
2. It is more important to correct an employee fault than to fix blame for it.
3. Employee performance is affected by problems both on the job and off.
4. Sudden or abrupt changes in behavior can be indications of important employee problems.
5. Problems should be dealt with as soon as possible after they are identified.
6. The attitude of the supervisor may have more to do with solving problems than the techniques of problem solving.
7. Correction of employee behavior should be resorted to only after the supervisor is sure that training or counseling will not be helpful.

8. Be sure to document your disciplinary actions.
9. Make sure that you are disciplining on the basis of facts rather than personal feelings.
10. Take each disciplinary step in order, being careful not to make snap judgments, or decisions based on impatience.

AA. Five Important Processes of Management

1. Planning
2. Organizing
3. Scheduling
4. Controlling
5. Motivating

BB. When the Supervisor Fails to Plan

1. Supervisor creates impression of not knowing his job
2. May lead to excessive overtime
3. Job runs itself—supervisor lacks control
4. Deadlines and appointments missed
5. Parts of the work go undone
6. Work interrupted by emergencies
7. Sets a bad example
8. Uneven workload creates peaks and valleys
9. Too much time on minor details at expense of more important tasks

CC. Fourteen General Principles of Management

1. Division of work
2. Authority and responsibility
3. Discipline
4. Unity of command
5. Unity of direction
6. Subordination of individual interest to general interest
7. Remuneration of personnel
8. Centralization
9. Scalar chain
10. Order
11. Equity
12. Stability of tenure of personnel
13. Initiative
14. Esprit de corps

DD. Change

Bringing about change is perhaps attempted more often, and yet less well understood, than anything else the supervisor does. How do people generally react to change? (People tend to resist change that is imposed upon them by other individuals or circumstances.

Change is characteristic of every situation. It is a part of every real endeavor where the efforts of people are concerned.

1. Why do people resist change?
   People may resist change because of:
   a. Fear of the unknown
   b. Implied criticism
   c. Unpleasant experiences in the past
   d. Fear of loss of status
   e. Threat to the ego
   f. Fear of loss of economic stability

2. How can we best overcome the resistance to change?
   In initiating change, take these steps:
   a. Get ready to sell
   b. Identify sources of help
   c. Anticipate objections
   d. Sell benefits
   e. Listen in depth
   f. Follow up

II. Brief Topical Summaries

A. Who/What is the Supervisor?
   1. The supervisor is often called the "highest level employee and the lowest level manager."
   2. A supervisor is a member of both management and the work group. He acts as a bridge between the two.
   3. Most problems in supervision are in the area of human relations, or people problems.
   4. Employees expect: Respect, opportunity to learn and to advance, and a sense of belonging, and so forth.
   5. Supervisors are responsible for directing people and organizing work. Planning is of paramount importance.
   6. A position description is a set of duties and responsibilities inherent to a given position.
   7. It is important to keep the position description up-to-date and to provide each employee with his own copy.

B. The Sociology of Work
   1. People are alike in many ways; however, each individual is unique.
   2. The supervisor is challenged in getting to know employee differences. Acquiring skills in evaluating individuals is an asset.
   3. Maintaining meaningful working relationships in the organization is of great importance.
   4. The supervisor has an obligation to help individuals to develop to their fullest potential.
   5. Job rotation on a planned basis helps to build versatility and to maintain interest and enthusiasm in work groups.
   6. Cross training (job rotation) provides backup skills.

7. The supervisor can help reduce tension by maintaining a sense of humor, providing guidance to employees, and by making reasonable and timely decisions. Employees respond favorably to working under reasonably predictable circumstances.
8. Change is characteristic of all managerial behavior. The supervisor must adjust to changes in procedures, new methods, technological changes, and to a number of new and sometimes challenging situations.
9. To overcome the natural tendency for people to resist change, the supervisor should become more skillful in initiating change.

C. Principles and Practices of Supervision

1. Employees should be required to answer to only one superior.
2. A supervisor can effectively direct only a limited number of employees, depending upon the complexity, variety, and proximity of the jobs involved.
3. The organizational chart presents the organization in graphic form. It reflects lines of authority and responsibility as well as interrelationships of units within the organization.
4. Distribution of work can be improved through an analysis using the "Work Distribution Chart."
5. The "Work Distribution Chart" reflects the division of work within a unit in understandable form.
6. When related tasks are given to an employee, he has a better chance of increasing his skills through training.
7. The individual who is given the responsibility for tasks must also be given the appropriate authority to insure adequate results.
8. The supervisor should delegate repetitive, routine work. Preparation of recurring reports, maintaining leave and attendance records are some examples.
9. Good discipline is essential to good task performance. Discipline is reflected in the actions of employees on the job in the absence of supervision.
10. Disciplinary action may have to be taken when the positive aspects of discipline have failed. Reprimand, warning, and suspension are examples of disciplinary action.
11. If a situation calls for a reprimand, be sure it is deserved and remember it is to be done in private.

D. Dynamic Leadership

1. A style is a personal method or manner of exerting influence.
2. Authoritarian leaders often see themselves as the source of power and authority.
3. The democratic leader often perceives the group as the source of authority and power.
4. Supervisors tend to do better when using the pattern of leadership that is most natural for them.
5. Social scientists suggest that the effective supervisor use the leadership style that best fits the problem or circumstances involved.
6. All four styles—telling, selling, consulting, joining—have their place. Using one does not preclude using the other at another time.

7. The theory X point of view assumes that the average person dislikes work, will avoid it whenever possible, and must be coerced to achieve organizational objectives.
8. The theory Y point of view assumes that the average person considers work to be a natural as play, and, when the individual is committed, he requires little supervision or direction to accomplish desired objectives.
9. The leader's basic assumptions concerning human behavior and human nature affect his actions, decisions, and other managerial practices.
10. Dissatisfaction among employees is often present, but difficult to isolate. The supervisor should seek to weaken dissatisfaction by keeping promises, being sincere and considerate, keeping employees informed, and so forth.
11. Constructive suggestions should be encouraged during the natural progress of the work.

E. Processes for Solving Problems

1. People find their daily tasks more meaningful and satisfying when they can improve them.
2. The causes of problems, or the key factors, are often hidden in the background. Ability to solve problems often involves the ability to isolate them from their backgrounds. There is some substance to the cliché that some persons "can't see the forest for the trees."
3. New procedures are often developed from old ones. Problems should be broken down into manageable parts. New ideas can be adapted from old one.
4. People think differently in problem-solving situations. Using a logical, patterned approach is often useful. One approach found to be useful includes these steps:
   a. Define the problem
   b. Establish objectives
   c. Get the facts
   d. Weigh and decide
   e. Take action
   f. Evaluate action

F. Training for Results

1. Participants respond best when they feel training is important to them.
2. The supervisor has responsibility for the training and development of those who report to him.
3. When training is delegated to others, great care must be exercised to insure the trainer has knowledge, aptitude, and interest for his work as a trainer.
4. Training (learning) of some type goes on continually. The most successful supervisor makes certain the learning contributes in a productive manner to operational goals.
5. New employees are particularly susceptible to training. Older employees facing new job situations require specific training, as well as having need for development and growth opportunities.
6. Training needs require continuous monitoring.
7. The training officer of an agency is a professional with a responsibility to assist supervisors in solving training problems.

8. Many of the self-development steps important to the supervisor's own growth are equally important to the development of peers and subordinates. Knowledge of these is important when the supervisor consults with others on development and growth opportunities.

G. Health, Safety, and Accident Prevention
1. Management-minded supervisors take appropriate measures to assist employees in maintaining health and in assuring safe practices in the work environment.
2. Effective safety training and practices help to avoid injury and accidents.
3. Safety should be a management goal. All infractions of safety which are observed should be corrected without exception.
4. Employees' safety attitude, training and instruction, provision of safe tools and equipment, supervision, and leadership are considered highly important factors which contribute to safety and which can be influenced directly by supervisors.
5. When accidents do occur, they should be investigated promptly for very important reasons, including the fact that information which is gained can be used to prevent accidents in the future.

H. Equal Employment Opportunity
1. The supervisor should endeavor to treat all employees fairly, without regard to religion, race, sex, or national origin.
2. Groups tend to reflect the attitude of the leader. Prejudice can be detected even in very subtle form. Supervisors must strive to create a feeling of mutual respect and confidence in every employee.
3. Complete utilization of all human resources is a national goal. Equitable consideration should be accorded women in the work force, minority-group members, the physically and mentally handicapped, and the older employee. The important question is: "Who can do the job?"
4. Training opportunities, recognition for performance, overtime assignments, promotional opportunities, and all other personnel actions are to be handled on an equitable basis.

I. Improving Communications
1. Communications is achieving understanding between the sender and the receiver of a message. It also means sharing information—the creation of understanding.
2. Communication is basic to all human activity. Words are means of conveying meanings; however, real meanings are in people.
3. There are very practical differences in the effectiveness of one-way, impersonal, and two-way communications. Words spoken face-to-face are better understood. Telephone conversations are effective, but lack the rapport of person-to-person exchanges. The whole person communicates.
4. Cooperation and communication in an organization go hand in hand. When there is a mutual respect between people, spelling out rules and procedures for communicating is unnecessary.
5. There are several barriers to effective communications. These include failure to listen with respect and understanding, lack of skill in feedback, and misinterpreting the meanings of words used by the speaker. It is also common

practice to listen to what we want to hear, and tune out things we do not want to hear.

6. Communication is management's chief problem. The supervisor should accept the challenge to communicate more effectively and to improve interagency and intra-agency communications.
7. The supervisor may often plan for and conduct meetings. The planning phase is critical and may determine the success or the failure of a meeting.
8. Speaking before groups usually requires extra effort. Stage fright may never disappear completely, but it can be controlled.

J. Self-Development

1. Every employee is responsible for his own self-development.
2. Toastmaster and toastmistress clubs offer opportunities to improve skills in oral communications.
3. Planning for one's own self-development is of vital importance. Supervisors know their own strengths and limitations better than anyone else.
4. Many opportunities are open to aid the supervisor in his developmental efforts, including job assignments; training opportunities, both governmental and non-governmental—to include universities and professional conferences and seminars.
5. Programmed instruction offers a means of studying at one's own rate.
6. Where difficulties may arise from a supervisor's being away from his work for training, he may participate in televised home study or correspondence courses to meet his self-development needs.

K. Teaching and Training

1. The Teaching Process

   Teaching is encouraging and guiding the learning activities of students toward established goals. In most cases this process consists of five steps: preparation, presentation, summarization, evaluation, and application.

   a. Preparation

      Preparation is two-fold in nature; that of the supervisor and the employee. Preparation by the supervisor is absolutely essential to success. He must know what, when, where, how, and whom he will teach. Some of the factors that should be considered are:

      1) The objectives
      2) The materials needed
      3) The methods to be used
      4) Employee participation
      5) Employee interest
      6) Training aids
      7) Evaluation
      8) Summarization

      Employee preparation consists in preparing the employee to receive the material. Probably the most important single factor in the preparation of the employee is arousing and maintaining his interest. He must know the objectives of the training, why he is there, how the material can be used, and its importance to him.

b. Presentation
In presentation, have a carefully designed plan and follow it. The plan should be accurate and complete, yet flexible enough to meet situations as they arise. The method of presentation will be determined by the particular situation and objectives.

c. Summary
A summary should be made at the end of every training unit and program. In addition, there may be internal summaries depending on the nature of the material being taught. The important thing is that the trainee must always be able to understand how each part of the new material relates to the whole.

d. Application
The supervisor must arrange work so the employee will be given a chance to apply new knowledge or skills while the material is still clear in his mind and interest is high. The trainee does not really know whether he has learned the material until he has been given a chance to apply it. If the material is not applied, it loses most of its value.

e. Evaluation
The purpose of all training is to promote learning. To determine whether the training has been a success or failure, the supervisor must evaluate this learning.
In the broadest sense, evaluation includes all the devices, methods, skills, and techniques used by the supervisor to keep himself and the employees informed as to their progress toward the objectives they are pursuing. The extent to which the employee has mastered the knowledge, skills, and abilities, or changed his attitudes, as determined by the program objectives, is the extent to which instruction has succeeded or failed.
Evaluation should not be confined to the end of the lesson, day, or program but should be used continuously. We shall note later the way this relates to the rest of the teaching process.

2. Teaching Methods
A teaching method is a pattern of identifiable student and instructor activity used in presenting training material.
All supervisors are faced with the problem of deciding which method should be used at a given time.

a. Lecture
The lecture is direct oral presentation of material by the supervisor. The present trend is to place less emphasis on the trainer's activity and more on that of the trainee.

b. Discussion
Teaching by discussion or conference involves using questions and other techniques to arouse interest and focus attention upon certain areas, and by doing so creating a learning situation. This can be one of the most

valuable methods because it gives the employees an opportunity to express their ideas and pool their knowledge.

c. Demonstration
The demonstration is used to teach how something works or how to do something. It can be used to show a principle or what the results of a series of actions will be. A well-staged demonstration is particularly effective because it shows proper methods of performance in a realistic manner.

d. Performance
Performance is one of the most fundamental of all learning techniques or teaching methods. The trainee may be able to tell how a specific operation should be performed but he cannot be sure he knows how to perform the operation until he has done so.
As with all methods, there are certain advantages and disadvantages to each method.

e. Which Method to Use
Moreover, there are other methods and techniques of teaching. It is difficult to use any method without other methods entering into it. In any learning situation, a combination of methods is usually more effective than any one method alone.

Finally, evaluation must be integrated into the other aspects of the teaching-learning process.

It must be used in the motivation of the trainees; it must be used to assist in developing understanding during the training; and it must be related to employee application of the results of training.

This is distinctly the role of the supervisor.

www.ingramcontent.com/pod-product-compliance
Lightning Source LLC
Chambersburg PA
CBHW080323020526
44117CB00035B/2640
* 9 7 8 1 7 9 9 3 4 7 8 4 2 *